THE R
IMPROVE

You can learn more from books—
perhaps even from one book—than
from all the universities in the world.

A. G. ELLIOT

THE RIGHT WAY
TO IMPROVE
YOUR ENGLISH

by
J. E. METCALFE

PAPERFRONTS

**ELLIOT RIGHT WAY BOOKS,
KINGSWOOD, SURREY, U.K.**

Made and printed by Richard Clay Ltd., Bungay, Suffolk.

CONTENTS

5

Prologue

A few years ago an illuminating report was published. This report was the work of a sub-committee, representing five universities, which had been set up to consider university entrance requirements, and in an appendix the members expressed deep concern at the low standard of use and understanding of English revealed by some candidates.

The following October the Dean of Westminster Medical School said that the standard of English shown in papers submitted at the entrance examination "bordered on illiteracy." The Dean said he could see no future in medicine for the candidate who could not express himself in speech and writing and who had not reinforced his background with wide reading. An official of the British Medical Association, agreeing with these remarks, said that many people tried to become doctors without any idea of the general education necessary.

If it is assumed that candidates for the universities, medical schools and other professional establishments represent the intellectual cream of English-speaking youth, what is to be concluded about the English of other young people? It is, unfortunately, easy to see that carelessness in English is one of our national shortcomings, a shortcoming, moreover, that few people worry about.

Carelessness is not the same as ignorance. An ignorant, illiterate person may be pitied for his deficiencies in English, which are no doubt due to his environment and mental limitations. Many a person who considers himself educated, however, who may have a rough idea of the basic principles of grammar, uses English carelessly, and persons of this kind, who are worse than the truly ignorant, deserve little sympathy.

School teachers are not always above reproach, and I have seen dreadful examples of carelessness by teachers of English. I wish that all who profess to "teach" English would realise that it is not a "subject" in itself but an integral part of everyday life, of

9

every branch of knowledge, learning, science, industry and business. This was the view of some of the members of the universities' sub-committee, who even felt that ability to understand and use English should not be tested by formal examinations.

This view is sound, but the idea would probably be impracticable. It is difficult to see what could adequately take the place of formal examinations, and, even if they were abolished, there would still have to be instruction in grammar, practice in the writing of prose, and a fostering of appreciation of literature and love of the English language for its own sake.

There is ample evidence that formal teaching of English is unsuccessful or insufficient. Bad English is with us everywhere, in our speech, in our correspondence, in business, in the Press, on the radio and on television. In this hasty age there may be no general encouragement towards better English, but many people, conscious of imperfection, like to help themselves to greater understanding. It is not only that they want to improve their English for the sake of personal satisfaction and enjoyment: they are rightly reluctant to run the risk of being branded as illiterate, semi-literate or careless.

Myself, I have long been irritated by the sorry state of affairs, and in desperation decided to write a book about it. The result, I hope, is not a dry and conventional text-book, but an informal series of chapters based on my experience of common weaknesses. Naturally I have had to go over some groundwork, too, but you will find that the groundwork is not divorced from reality.

English, as we have seen, should not be regarded as a "subject," and a book on English, therefore, need not be the work of a pedagogic specialist. My professional interests happen to be scientific, but my enthusiasm for English springs from a lifelong love of the language and its literature and from many years of practical experience in writing about a variety of topics.

I hesitate to refer in almost the same breath to a much greater writer who was no specialist, either—Sir Winston Churchill, a man of many parts. In *My Early Life* Sir Winston wrote: "I would make all boys learn English . . . the only thing I would whip them for is not knowing English."

Even if you cannot be whipped, I hope this book will help you to *Improve Your English*.

J. E. METCALFE.

CHAPTER I

On English

◆◆◆

WHAT is good English? The shortest answer to this question is probably "English which is grammatical." It is by no means the complete answer, however, for a prose passage can be grammatically correct but stultified by such faults as weakness in the choice and order of words, using many more words than are necessary, going a long way round to say something (circumlocution), using well-worn and overworked groups of words (clichés), ambiguity, padding and imprecision.

Grammar is the basis of a language, the framework on which ideas are hung, and the loftiest imagery of thought can fall flat if ungrammatically expressed. The rebel will argue that grammar is just a set of rules, and that as language is primarily for the conveyance of thought, for communication, it matters little how he says or writes something as long as his meaning is understood. The rebel might also ask: "Who made the rules, anyway?"

This is a weak argument, for grammar exists in any language long before the language comes to be written. Some of the more common West African languages, for example, are now written, but when the missionary scholars first tackled the task of putting them on paper they found the problem of grammar the hardest problem of all. The grammar of each of these languages is more complex than that of English, not only in the verbs and the construction of sentences but also in the use of nouns, and no doubt the unwritten languages of West Africa (a region of which I have some experience) are just as formal. If, then, primitive people find it necessary to have grammar, is it not more necessary for races which claim to be relatively civilised?

11

THE NEED FOR GRAMMAR

In all phases of human life there is a need, indeed a desire, for discipline, a need which helps to distinguish us from animals. One of the most important features of our life is language, spoken or written, and there is no need to dwell on a picture of human life without the benefit of language. The discipline of language is the thing called grammar, and for anyone to protest that grammar is unnecessary, or can be relaxed at will, shows himself to be unduly conceited or mentally lazy.

Who made the rules? The speakers of a language have made the rules, through custom, usage and logic, even if at times the logic appears to be curious. There has been an urge, especially important in law, to distinguish between shades of meaning. There has been a wish to avoid tiresome queries and explanations between two persons in conversation. There has been anxiety to express much in little. There has been, above all, the unconscious human desire for orderliness, for that discipline to which I have alluded, and the discipline has embraced the other desirable qualities of communication to form grammar.

THE ENGLISH LANGUAGE

Broadly, English grammar is based on the grammars of the languages from which English is derived. The earliest source was the old Anglo-Saxon, or Germanic, so called from the Angli, a Germanic tribe which settled in Britain in the fifth and sixth centuries, and it is strange that the original languages of these islands survive only in the Celtic and Cymric tongues, such as Gaelic and Welsh.

Scholars added Latin, and in the eleventh century the Danes brought Scandinavian. The Normans introduced a great deal of French to the language, and *The Canterbury Tales* show that in Chaucer's time (1340-1400) Southern English consisted of Anglo-Saxon and Old French. The philosophers and scientists introduced a number of Greek and Arabic words, while the musicians and artists gave us some Italian and Dutch. Later, explorers and their men brought words from the East, from India, China and Malaya.

The English language is thus a hotch-potch of other languages, and the gradual changes have divided its history into three chronological periods known as Old English, Middle English and Modern English. The Old English period is considered to have ended about 1150 and the Middle English period about 1500, by which time the convergent streams had united to form Modern English, which is virtually the English of today.

Since 1500 there have been changes in literary and conversational style, changes in usage, changes in the meanings of words, changes in spelling, and changes in the order of words ("syntax"), but grammar has hardly changed at all. The fundamental rules now observed and to be respected, in fact, are the rules observed by the Elizabethan writers.

THE GRAMMAR OF WRITERS

In discussing English grammar we assume it to be mainly the grammar of prose. In great poetry and in good verse, however, it is remarkable how, in spite of scansion (page 158), rhyme, and the order of words and phrases, little or no grammatical fault can be found, and refuge is taken in "poetic licence" infrequently. Poetry is not meant to be strictly analysed —pulling a poem to bits was an invention of the pedagogues— but, if it is, it is usually found to consist of a series of grammatically-constructed sentences. Analysis of much modern experimental poetry and verse would be less rewarding.

Somebody is now sure to ask why, if grammar is considered to be so important, many celebrated writers of published works do not bother about it, and celebrated writers of published works should be the leaders. The answer is that the number of distinguished prose-writers who turn out ungrammatical work is very small in relation to the number of the orthodox.

The ungrammatical army can be divided into those who write carelessly and those who deliberately flout the regulations. Those who write carelessly would probably realise and admit their lapses, but publishers' readers are usually too busy to point out mistakes. There is also evidence, I regret to say, of some shameful ignorance among writers, but I prefer not to dwell on it.

Then we come to the rebels, those who cock a snoot at the discipline of grammar, who, among the writers of prose, are confined to novelists. By rebel novelists I mean those few who try to follow patterns set by James Joyce and Gertrude Stein, as well as others, somewhat more orthodox, of the school of Ernest Hemingway.

The method of the first set can perhaps be described briefly as an attempt to commit ideas and thoughts to paper without the benefit of language—that is, without formal grammar—and I think a parallel could be drawn between this method of writing and the picture-strip way of telling a story. Writers of the second set, unlike those of the first set, present a coherent narrative, but in doing so reduce structure, sentences, words and grammar to a minimum.

I shall not try to defend these schools of novelists in their treatment of the English language. At their best they are interesting for a limited time, occasionally they have sparkling wit to offer, sometimes their "stream of consciousness" psychology is startlingly profound, and a few works of these schools have established places in twentieth-century literature. At their worst they are fit only for burlesque. In short, schools of novelists are not necessarily schools of English.

A welcome change from the despisers of grammar can be afforded by consideration of the splendid array of writers who respect good English, or did so when they were alive. Most of them are "mute, inglorious" Miltons, writing daily in peaceful anonymity or under insignificant names. And even if we were to make a list of well-known writers, novelists, journalists, essayists and others—in whose work little grammatical fault could be found, the list would be pleasingly long.

I have brought authors into my case for grammar simply because their writings can be read by all, and not because I am primarily addressing those who aspire to authorship. We all have to do a certain amount of writing today, writing that is not intended for publication, and these notes are for the guidance of those who know they are hazy about English and want to improve, those who think they are writing good English but would be surprised at their numerous mistakes, and those who are interested in the English language for its own sake.

SPOKEN ENGLISH

Most of us, too, have to do a great deal of talking, but speech is different from writing. It is so ephemeral that some minor errors of construction are often overlooked, and many conversations, if put into cold print, would shock by their apparent immaturity of language. Besides the minor errors of construction there are other common errors which outrage the sensitive ear and constitute social solecisms, such as "Between you and I" and "He ought to, didn't he?"

English pronunciation varies not only between the different English-speaking countries but also—most of all, in fact— between the different regions of our own small islands, and, within reason, you can pronounce words as you please as long as your pronunciation is acceptable. Matters of pronunciation, therefore, will have no place in this book. But grammar is rigid, and no accepted god likes to be accused of having feet of clay.

THE PREVALENCE OF POOR ENGLISH

Before concluding the chapter I think it would be interesting to consider the reasons for the present widespread weakness in English. One reason, of course, is the inability of many people to think logically, for grammar and punctuation are largely based on logic which in turn is based on fundamental linguistic premises.

Another reason is found in lazy reading habits. Comparatively few people read at all, the bulk of the masses being semiliterate in spite of compulsory "education." Far too many people confine their "reading" to strip pictures, illustrated papers, and the more sensational and moronic newspapers, and it is not surprising that they hardly know what a sentence looks like.

Of those people who can and do read, many do so unintelligently, taking in the general sense without looking at the words or thinking about the construction of the sentences. A person who is brought up to love books and respect authorship will naturally take an interest in the way things are written, will gradually come to recognise good writing, and will try to instil the essential qualities into his own writing, no matter what sort of writing he may be doing.

We tend towards carelessness, unfortunately, and even those who normally write grammatically and tolerably well sometimes make mistakes. The most respected writers can nod occasionally. Many people write too hastily, but the world of work is such that few people in their ordinary business take time to revise anything they have written. Dictation is an enemy of good writing, and should be restricted to the preparation of a first draft which must be painstakingly amended by hand before the final version is produced. It is a pity that in business there is seldom time for such striving after perfection.

Of the most eminent writers in this streamlined age, few practise dictation. When you read something that is smooth, measured and rhythmic, with the right word here and the right phrase there, do not imagine that the passage was written straight off like a post-card message. A celebrated writer (I think it was G. K. Chesterton) once said that easy reading meant hard writing; that is a truth which has to be learnt, but it is certainly worth the learning and should be taken to heart.

WHAT IS BAD ENGLISH?

If I have not given the complete answer to the question with which this chapter started—"What is good English?"—I can at least give you some examples of bad English. Read the following:

"Who shall I give it to?"

"He very kindly promised to take my sister and I for a sail."

"You will see perfectly if you stand here beside we fellows."

"The hotel has wash-basins in every room."

"The seeds should be set in rows with two feet between each."

"Neither the manager nor his assistant were there at nine o'clock."

"Either the British or the American Governments should be represented."

"All the houses have a television aerial."

"Get it over quick."

"It would have been better to have ignored him."

"The neighbours thought him a wealthy man. Which, of course, he wasn't."

"Due to the illness of the chairman, the meeting was cancelled."

"The reason for the attack on his rival was because of pent-up ill-feeling."

"Under the circumstances his resignation was justified."

"I can't face up to those kind of things."

"Do you think that wall is perpendicular?"

"The subsoil is underlaid by a layer of sandstone."

"This strata is somewhat porous."

"It was a wet day, but I took an umbrella."

"I had no idea you were all that good at singing."

"Can you loan me a fiver, old man?"

"After the holidays I will go back to work feeling a new man."

"Shall you join us in the bar?"

"Do you really want to forego the privilege?"

"His forbears were men of war."

"I scanned the paper while I was shaving."

"Referring to your letter, the animal has already been slaughtered."

"Broadly speaking, women are more suited to routine jobs than men."

"Providing the weather is suitable, the race will take place on Saturday."

"That story, I promise, was perfectly true."

"Though shy, most people find him good company."

Every one of those examples has something wrong with it. If you do not know why, you will find out in the course of this book.

CHAPTER II

Parts of Speech

＊＊＊＊＊＊＊＊＊＊＊＊＊＊＊＊＊＊＊＊＊＊＊＊＊＊＊＊＊＊＊＊＊＊

I find that in order to write about good English properly I have to get right back to fundamentals. I *could* give a bald list of rules of grammar and a list of examples of bad English and good English, but this method would not help you to understand why certain things are right and other things are wrong.

The title of the chapter may sound elementary to some of my readers, who perhaps will feel I am insulting them by bothering to write about something everybody is supposed to have learnt at school. But if these readers bear with me, and read on, they will be surprised to find how much more there is about parts of speech than they ever realised in their schooldays. I have surprised myself, in fact, by discovering the increasing fascination of something that is usually taken for granted.

DEFINITIONS

Nearly every word in the English language can be classified into its kind, the different kinds of words being known as "parts of speech." It is too late to ask at this stage why classifications into fixed kinds are necessary, the classifications having become crystallised through centuries of linguistic discipline. In any case, as will be seen, the various parts of speech are not always firmly fixed.

The following are the parts of speech:—

Nouns;	Pronouns;
Verbs;	Conjunctions;
Adjectives;	Prepositions;
Adverbs;	Interjections.

Unfortunately the classifications are not perfect.

Most words are easy to classify—that is, you know at a glance which part of speech a word belongs to—but some words can belong to two or more parts of speech. It frequently happens that a word cannot readily be classified at all; for example, it can form part of a phrase that, of little or no meaning in itself, has become understandable only through the common usage of years or centuries. Such use of a word or phrase, constituting an *idiom*, is said to be idiomatic.

Of all eight parts of speech, the most tantalising are pronouns. Although there is no question about the principal pronouns, it must be admitted that this classification has somewhat hazy boundaries and there can be much vagueness about words which lie near the frontiers.

AN ANALYSIS

In the following descriptions of parts of speech it will often be necessary to wander from the main stream of discussion to examine the curiosities of individual words, as this is the most suitable part of the book for such detailed diversions. Before proceeding, however, let us, as an interesting exercise, consider one of my sentences and try to classify each of its words.

"It frequently happens that a word cannot readily be classified at all."

It: Pronoun, but the use here is idiomatic.

Frequently: Adverb.

Happens: Verb.

That: Relative pronoun, but the use here is idiomatic.

A: Adjective; indefinite article. (See page 24.)

Word: Noun.

Cannot . . . be classified: Verb (actually a combination of verbs, or "compound verb").

Readily: Adverb.

At all: Idiomatic.

Thus in this one sentence, chosen at random, it is not possible to classify firmly *every* word into an appropriate part of speech, but for a true understanding of the language parts of speech must be studied.

NOUNS

Nouns are just *things*, animate or inanimate, real or imaginary, visible or invisible. English has the advantage that inanimate things are of neuter gender; that is, they are not masculine or feminine as they are, for example, in French.

Proper nouns are names of people, places, oceans, ships, racehorses, streets, and so forth. A proper noun (except in the case of a few peculiar surnames) always starts with a capital letter.

PLURALS

Most plurals in English consist of the singular form with the addition of *s*, with or without some modification. One modification is the *-ies* form for words ending in *y*, as in *sky* (*skies*), *cry* (*cries*).

Words ending in *o* take *-es*, as in *grotto* (*grottoes*), *echo* (*echoes*), *salvo* (*salvoes*). In old writings you may come across *grotto's*, but there is no justification for the apostrophe.

Exceptions to the *s* system of plurals—exceptions which certainly add to the fascination of English—are words like *man*, *tooth*, *foot*, *mouse*, and *child*. *Brethren*, the old form for *brothers*, is now mostly used in a figurative sense.

Foreign words which have firmly become established in the language may or may not take the foreign plural. The Italian *solo*, for instance, can become *soloes* or *soli*. French is well-enough known in this country, however, to justify *tableaux* and *bureaux*.

Latin nouns usually retain their Latin plurals, thus:—

-um	into	*-a*
stratum		strata
datum		data
minimum		minima
spectrum		spectra
-us	into	*-i*
radius		radii
hippopotamus		hippopotami
tumulus		tumuli
-a	into	*-ae*
larva		larvae
nebula		nebulae
abscissa		abscissae

There is no great wrong in writing or saying *stratums* or *radiuses*. The unforgivable sin is to use the plural where a singular is intended, and of depressing frequency is the horrid habit of referring to "this strata of rock" and even "these stratas." Three other plurals which are commonly misused as singular nouns are *media, data* and *phenomena* instead of *medium, data* and *phenomenon*. Particularly prevalent is "this data" (in the sense of information or knowledge) instead of "these data."

Hippopotamus is a Latin word derived from the Greek word ending in *-os*. Yet *rhinoceros,* strangely, has kept its Greek form, and the plural should be *rhinoceroses*. Sportsmen, however, have a pleasant little convention of dropping the endings from animal plurals, and hence they shoot or bag pheasant and grouse. This use of the singular for the plural is a commendable practice when properly applied, especially in such quantitative terms as *gross*.

Incidentally, many editors, publishers and printers, to avoid contention, make a practice of agreeing upon definite abbreviations to be used for terms of quantity whether singular or plural. Thus, in writing anything for publication, you might anticipate the editor's blue pencil by using *mm., cm., km., kg., oz.* and *lb.*

In this connection, it should be noted that *ozs.* and *lbs.* are both wrong. *Oz.* merely represents the pharmacist's squiggle for *ounce* or *ounces. Lb.* is short for the Latin *libra* (plural *librae*).

Of the plurals of nouns and names which themselves end with *s,* many people have hazy ideas. Such nouns are *lens, iris,* and *gas,* and such proper nouns (names) are *Jones, Francis,* and *Jenkins*. To make such words plural, simply add *-es*. "The Jenkinses went out to dinner" is perfectly correct.

Exceptions are *means* and *news*. We talk about "this means" and "these means," but *news* is always regarded as singular.

POSSESSIVES

Ownership, or a "belonging to," is signified by a possessive, which usually, in the case of a single possessor, is denoted by the "apostrophe *s*." I make no apology for bringing up this apparently elementary subject, for too often the grammatical rules of possession are ignored or unknown.

The singular cases are those like "Jim's dog," "The curate's egg," and "St. John's Church." "One week's time" also demands a possessive. If a proper noun ends in *s* the rule is still applied; thus, the correct forms are "St. James's Street," "Frances's doll," and "Columbus's ship."

Where ownership or the "belonging to" is shared by two or more nouns, the joint possession is usually indicated by "*s* apostrophe," as in "The boys' hats," "The dogs' bones" and "The two nations' mutual understanding."

Collective nouns are treated as singular, and the apostrophe comes before the *s*. Examples are: "The children's toys," "The people's homes," "The men's work" and "The mice's hole."

I have already referred to the implied possession of "One week's time," the justification lying in the fact that the phrase means the length of time belonging to one week. Similarly we can have "In two weeks' time" or "A hundred years' time." But remember that the apostrophe must not be used if you omit the word "time" and simply say something like "In two weeks I shall be twenty-one."

An astonishingly large number of bad mistakes is made when people's homes are being written about. When you say, "I went to the Johnstones'," you mean you went to the home not of Mr. Johnstone or Mrs. Johnstone but of both Johnstones, so that "the Johnstones'" is just an abbreviation of "the Johnstones' home." It is equally simple if your friends' name ends in *s*, in which case you write: "I went to the Joneses'," or "I went to the Inglises'."

In spite of the simplicity of this kind of possessive, mistakes appear in print almost every day, mistakes that are evidence of cloudy mentality.

An interesting use of the possessive is in references to the names of firms. If you want to write to tell someone where you bought your curtains you can say: "I bought my curtains at Smith's" or ". . . . at Smiths'," meaning, of course, Smith's or Smiths' shop. If the firm is run by one man called Smith it is correct to write "Smith's," but if the firm is big enough to be controlled by a few of the Smith family then "Smiths'" is correct. If you do not know how many Smiths there are, or how big the firm is, you are on the safe side if you write "Smith's."

Many firms and organisations, regrettably, have dropped the

possessive. "Lloyds Bank Plc," for example, is the official form under which the company is registered.

VERBS

Verbs are the words that indicate *action*, a doing of something. Thus, in the simple sentences, "I go," "He had," "She will come," the verbs are *go*, *had* and *will come*.

When it is desired to talk or write about a verb in its general sense, it is usual to add the preposition *to*, and the form *to eat* (and so forth) is termed the *infinitive*.

In one way verbs are the most important of the parts of speech, for, as you will see in a later chapter (Chapter VI), every true sentence must contain a verb. There is so much to know about verbs and their use, in fact, that they will form the subject of a special chapter (Chapter IV).

ADJECTIVES

Adjectives are words that qualify nouns. They describe what kinds of things they are, or which things they are. Common adjectives are *big, pretty, sour, young, best*.

Adjectives include personal titles, such as *Mr.*, *Mrs.* and *Miss*, *Sir* and *Lord*, where the name immediately follows. In "The Duke of . . . ," on the other hand, *Duke* is a noun.

Adjectives include those of possession: *my, your, his, her, our, their*. For the sake of emphasis, the possessive adjective is sometimes followed by *own*, as in "my own hat," when *own* also becomes an adjective.

These words can also be grouped under the classification of "possessive pronouns," but as they are selective, in saying *whose* things are meant, the words are also adjectives. The allied forms *mine, yours, theirs*, however, which cannot precede a noun, and which imply "my hat," "your . . . ," or "their . . . ," are definitely pronouns.

Adjectives include such vague expressions as *numerous, innumerable, few, no* (meaning not any), where the expression directly precedes the noun.

There are exceptional cases, of course, where the adjective follows the noun, but such cases are usually found only in special literary constructions, in poetical language, and in oratory. The beginning of Milton's *Lycidas* is but one example:

> "Yet once more, O ye laurels, and once more
> Ye myrtles brown, with ivy never sere,
> I come to pluck your berries harsh and crude,
> And with forced fingers rude
> Shatter your leaves before the mellowing year."

Adjectives include colours, numerals, and nationalities. There is often some difficulty in deciding whether to use a capital *F* in such everyday things as "French chalk," "French window," and "French polish." It is often considered that, as the French origin has got lost in the vortex of common English usage, a small *f* will do. But as the word *French* deserves a capital in its own right, it is as well to use it always.

Adjectives include the "articles," which for the sake of convenience will be described in a separate section.

ARTICLES

The adjectives *a* and *an* are called the "indefinite articles," while the adjective *the*, for obvious reasons, is called the "definite article."

There has been an unjustified tendency in recent years to write and speak of "an hotel," as if the *h* were silent. I have not traced the origin of this ungainly custom, but if you want to write and speak good English do not be afraid of "a hotel."

Think of all the nouns you can starting with a sounded ("aspirate") *h*. Do you prefix them with *an*? Of course not. Where the *h* is silent, as in *honour*, *hour*, the article *an* is correct.

Another strange tendency is to write "an unique article," instead of "a unique article," which most people actually say. This, too, is incomprehensible, for nobody would write about "an unicorn."

I shall conclude my notes on articles by drawing attention to a vulgar practice of the less responsible newspapers and periodicals. This is the inexcusable omission of the definite article *the* at the beginning of a sentence, clause or phrase, and I pray you not to be misled by this custom into thinking it is good English.

ADVERBS

Adverbs qualify verbs as adjectives qualify nouns. Thus, while a verb tells you about the doing of something, an adverb tells you how it is done. Most adverbs consist of adjectives followed by the suffix *-ly*, as in *quickly*, *cleverly*, *cautiously*, *willingly*.

Not all adverbs end in *-ly*. *How* itself is an adverb. So is *well*, as in "He does it well." *Fast* and *hard* are two common examples, and these, incidentally, are words which can be both adverbs and adjectives.

In the short imperative sentence, "Run fast," *fast* is an adverb. ("Imperative" implies a command, an order.) And yet, if we say "We had a fast run," *fast* is an adjective. It is similar with *hard* which is an adverb in "Hit him hard" but an adjective in "I took a hard knock."

The adverb *hardly* has a different meaning from the adverb *hard*. *Hardly* means "scarcely," "nearly," "not quite," and is probably connected with the archaic (old-fashioned) *hard* meaning "near." "He lives hard by the church" used to be common usage.

There are some words which are classified as adverbs largely because they are nearer to adverbs than they are to any other part of speech. Examples of such "adverbs" are *where*, *there*, *whatever* and *however*. In so far as these words qualify verbs—as in "You put it there," and "I did it, however"—they are adverbs, but the point is a technical one and we need spend no more time on it.

Adverbs can also qualify adjectives and even other adverbs. Examples of these uses are:—

Adverb qualifying adjective.
"You are extremely kind."
"It is a ridiculously simple problem."
Adverb qualifying adverb.
"He did it remarkably quickly."
"How well you draw!"

Adverbs can qualify participles, as in "I am greatly pleased." But in mentioning participles I am anticipating Chapter IV. Before that stage is reached we have to discuss more parts of speech.

CHAPTER III

More Parts of Speech

◆◆

IN the list of parts of speech on page 18 adverbs are followed by pronouns. So much can be written about pronouns, however, that they demand a chapter to themselves, and accordingly our study of them will be deferred until Chapter V. The next three parts of speech on our list, then, are conjunctions, prepositions and interjections, all of which will be dealt with in this chapter.

CONJUNCTIONS

Before starting I should explain two terms. A *clause* is a complete statement, forming part of a sentence, which contains a verb; it may, in fact, be a short sentence. A *phrase*, on the other hand (contrary to common belief), does not include a verb. This matter will be discussed in more detail in Chapter VI.

Very often a sentence is composed of two or more shorter sentences or clauses which must be joined in some way. Consider the following.

"The night was dark *and* it was cold."

"The night was cold *but* there was no fire."

"Nero played *while* Rome burned."

Each clause in each of these sentences is self-sufficient. It could be written on its own. Yet to avoid jerkiness in construction and ensure a smoother flow the different pairs of clauses are linked by the words *and*, *but* and *while*. These words are conjunctions.

SELECTION OF CONJUNCTIONS

Conjunctions, besides linking parts of a sentence, also express something in themselves.

In the first example above, the second clause, after *and*, simply continues the emotion evoked by the darkness of the night. The conjunction *but*, however, signifies a contrast between the two clauses of the second sentence. The same effect could be produced by saying: "*Although* the night was cold there was no fire." There will be a more detailed discussion of *but* later in the chapter.

A skilfully-applied conjunction, then, not only serves its primary purpose of joining parts of a sentence together, but also pays a contribution—sometimes quite an important contribution—to the general sense of the sentence. This subject will be dealt with more fully in Chapter VI. Meanwhile it may be useful to list the more common conjunctions, which are:—

And	Because (As, For, Since)
But (Yet)	Or
While	If
Although (Though)	

The words in brackets in the list are usually, but not necessarily, alternative forms.

STARTING SENTENCES

In spite of schoolday admonitions against starting a sentence with *And* or *But*, there is nothing pernicious in the practice provided it is kept under proper control. There is very good precedent, in fact, in the Old Testament, where innumerable verses start with either of these two words.

When a sentence starts with *But*, a contrast with the preceding sentence is implied.

And and *But*, however, are the only conjunctions with which you can start a simple sentence. (A simple sentence is a sentence without a secondary sentence or clause.)

Try starting a simple sentence with any of the other conjunctions in the above list. You will find it is incomplete without another statement to follow or precede it.

"While John was weeding the garden."

"Although it was raining."

"Since (As, Because) it was Wednesday."

"Or you can have this one."

"If I were you." (*Not* "If I was you." See Chapter IV, "The Subjunctive.")

Without the conjunction at the beginning, each of these sentences makes sense; but with the conjunction, it is left hanging in the air.

Thus, apart from *and* and *but*, all conjunctions require at least two clauses to be linked together. Sometimes you may come across *Or* used at the beginning of a sentence, but on inspection you will probably find that the preceding sentence has finished too early.

Do not be confused if you find *Though* or *Although* used at the beginning of a sentence and *apparently* without a supporting sentence, as in:

"Though sick, he was able to work."
This really means: "He was able to work though he was sick."

In the first sentence, the words "he was" are *understood*. "Understood" parts of a sentence are very common in the English language, but the trouble is that some people lose track of what is "understood."

CONJUNCTIVE PHRASES

Besides words of conjunction, there are also conjunctive phrases, such as "despite the fact that," "owing to the fact that," "for the reason that," and "in addition to which." These are somewhat clumsy, and come under the heading of "circumlocution." Usually there is no reason why such phrases should not be replaced by single words. Thus, in the examples given, the first could be replaced by *although*, the second and third by *as* or *because*, and the fourth by *and*.

A NOTE ON "AND"

Some newspapers and periodicals, in those parts which are not "text"—that is, for instance, in headlines, captions to illustrations, summaries, advertisements, book lists and share lists—make a practice of printing a comma for *and*, on the assumption that the word is understood.

This is done only to save space, but in my opinion the comma is an unfortunate alternative as it has a meaning of its own which is not necessarily the meaning of *and*. In any case the amount of space saved is so small that one wonders if the substitution is worth while. If the sub-editor is so short of room that an *and* cannot be squeezed in, more use could surely be made of the unambiguous sign "&", which, incidentally, is called the "ampersand."

"BUT"

In the use of *but* as a conjunction it is essential that the two connected statements are in contrast to one another. I have given as an example: "The night was cold but there was no fire."

That is right; but often you see *but* used wrongly, where there is no contrast or where the contrast is already expressed. Consider the sentence:

"He did not die, but he recovered and lived to a ripe old age."

If he did not die he must have recovered, so that there is no contrast after *but*. The word is therefore misused. If, however, we simply replace *but* by *and*, the sentence is clumsy. It would be better to reconstruct the sentence and say: "He did not die; he recovered and lived to a ripe old age."

A similar case is:

"In vain I tried, but I failed."

If I tried in vain it is obvious that I failed; therefore, either *in vain* must be dropped or *but* must be replaced by *and*.

You can fall into a trap here if you are not careful. I hope I have explained the use of *but* as a contrasting conjunction between two clauses or statements in a sentence. *But*, however, can also be used to indicate a contrast between opposing *words*—for example, between two adjectives, two nouns, or two verbs.

Correct examples are:—

"It is not hot but cold."

"It is not a dog but a cat."

"He is not coming but going."

This is the trap. Although these examples are right the following examples are wrong, because *but* neutralises factors which are already opposed:—

"It is not hot but it is cold."

"It is not a dog but it is a cat."

"He is not coming but he is going."

If you want to repeat "it is" in each case, the *but* should be replaced by a semi-colon. The former construction, however, is preferable.

"BUT" AS "EXCEPT"

The use of *but* to mean *except* is common. Consider the sentence: "Nobody knows but me." Is this right or wrong?

We must first decide whether *but* is intended as a preposition or a conjunction. If a preposition is intended, then the objective *me* is correct. (The meaning of "objective" will be explained in Chapter VI.)

If, however, a conjunction is intended, the sentence is probably a shortening of "Nobody knows, but I know," and in this, even though the sentence does not strictly make sense, *I* is right.

If our assumption is correct, that the sentence is abbreviated, then *I* is subjective. (I apologise for anticipating some of the material for Chapter VI, but it seems to be necessary.) There are other cases, nevertheless, where no assumption need be made as there is no doubt about the matter.

"The boy stood on the burning deck
Whence all but he had fled."

The phrase "all but he" is the subject preceding the verb "had fled," and the use of *he* is correct. Think how discordant the line would sound if Felicia Hemans had written (in "Casabianca") "Whence all but him had fled."

Thus, when we know definitely whether we are dealing with subject or object, there is no doubt about the "case" following *but*. For example:

Subjective case—"Everyone but I went home."
Objective case—"They gave some to everyone but me."

But *where doubt exists*—and it often does—it is an idiomatic custom to assume that *but* (meaning *except*) is a preposition and therefore followed by the objective case.

A rather odd use of *but* which might be mentioned here is in such constructions as: "Who knows but that the old man was the culprit after all?" In such sentences *that* is sometimes replaced by *what*, but as the whole construction is idiomatic it does not matter much.

This kind of language is permissible if used sparingly in conversation. It is apt to get out of control when used by the woolly-minded, and we hear confused absurdities like: "Who knows but what the old man was not the culprit after all?"

"SINCE," "FOR," "AS"

The three words *since*, *for* and *as* can mean the same as (or are *synonymous* with) *because*, and it is in this connection that they are used as conjunctions. In the following sentence all four are of equal value:—

"I went home $\begin{cases} \text{because} \\ \text{since} \\ \text{for} \\ \text{as} \end{cases}$ it was obvious I was needed."

These three words, however, have other functions, too.

Probably the commonest application of *since* is as a preposition, as in: "He has not been home since Christmas." *For*, too, is commonest as a preposition, and prepositions will form the subject of our next section.

I said "commonest *as* a preposition." What is this use of *as*? Here, it means "according to the manner of." In this use it frankly cannot be designated as being a member of any particular part of speech, any more than it can be classified in such sentences as:

"It shone as brightly as the sun."

"He is as happy as a king."

In the next chapter you will come across the *subjunctive* mood of a verb, which I have already mentioned. I need not explain this now, but you are using the subjunctive in saying things like: "I felt as if I were dreaming."

The word *as* can also mean *like* in the sense of being "similar to." "He is as a child" means the same as "He is like a child." It is used as *also*, or *too*, in the phrase "as well," where the word *well* is equally meaningless. "I am coming as well."

An extension of this idiom is provided by such constructions as: "Jim is coming as well as Jack," where "as well as" means "in addition to."

Truly, *as* is a tantalising little word, but a word of great utility.

PREPOSITIONS

A preposition is a word which expresses the relationship of one word with another, usually (but not always) of a noun, a pronoun, or a participle. (Participles are explained in Chapter IV.)

In the phrase "in the house," *in* is a preposition used to express the relationship of a noun with something else. Other examples of prepositions with nouns are: "*near* the stream," "*with* a will," "*by* hook or *by* crook."

Examples of prepositions with pronouns are: "*to* you," "*from* me," "*with* them."

Examples of prepositions with present participles are: "*without* going," "*by* living," "*beyond* walking."

Here is a list of other prepositions:

of	off	below	across
for	up	above	beside
outside	down	beneath	toward(s)
outwith	before	around	along
(Scottish)	after	past	among(st)
inside	under	till (until)	amid(st)
on	over	abreast (of)	unto

No doubt you will be able to think of many more.

Most of us remember prepositions because at school we were taught it was wrong to end a sentence (or a clause in a sentence) with a preposition. The foundation of this belief may have been the apparent meaning of the word *preposition* itself, signifying "before *position*."

The word, however, is unfortunate, and to interpret it literally would be tantamount to adjusting the language to suit its meaning—for, after all, the language is older than the term "preposition." Let us now examine the matter more closely.

THE PLACING OF PREPOSITIONS

There used to be a silly maxim something like this: "It is wrong to use a preposition to end a sentence with." There is no grammatical fault with this sentence, but it sounds clumsy. Such a remark could be expressed: "It is wrong to use a preposition for ending a sentence." (Note: *for ending* is an example of a preposition with a present participle.)

The placing of a preposition depends to some extent on the type of writing or speech in which it is to be used. "There is the boy I gave the toffee to" sounds freer, less pedantic, than "There is the boy to whom I gave the toffee."

What is suitable for a casual remark, however, may not be suitable, for example, for a statesman's speech. Consider the following:

"The fate of this great nation, of whom it might be said that at no time in two thousand years has she attempted to shirk her responsibilities, is today hanging by a slender thread. There are countries to whom she has offered the hand of friendship. There are countries to whom she has gladly given every help in time of war. These things shall surely not go unregarded. The world is ever growing smaller, and the tremendous continents between which the mighty seas roll unceasingly are drawing ever closer together. It behoves us all, therefore, to stand together in brotherhood, so that, when the time comes, we shall not be wanting for support. But with what are our friends to support us? Never fear. They have the spiritual resources of centuries."

There are several prepositions in that passage, not one of which falls at the end of a sentence or the end of a clause. The only sentence that might, I think, be improved by a shunting of the preposition is that containing *with:* "But what are our friends to support us with?"

Ending a sentence (or a clause in a sentence) with a preposition may not sound elegant, and it may offend you, but in that case you can reconstruct; that is, you can rearrange the sentence in such a way that the use of a preposition is avoided.

If the sense of a sentence or clause, however, demands that a preposition be placed at the end, and the result is harmonious, then put the preposition there.

UNSUPPORTED PREPOSITIONS

Frequently a preposition can be used alone, without a noun, pronoun, or participle, but in all such cases the supporting word is understood. In the following examples the understood words are in brackets:

B

"I saw three ships come sailing by (the shore)."
"There is a man outside (the door)."
"I am going in (the house)."
"The doctor has gone up (the stairs)."
A little reflection will suggest innumerable examples of this type.

PREPOSITIONS AS ADJECTIVES

Occasionally a preposition is used as an adjective, as in *up train*, *down train*, *inside berth*, *outside seat*, *under dog*, and *past president*.

"TO" AND ITS OMISSION

Let me give you some good advice on the use of the preposition *to*. You can go *to* places, but never "go places," unless the place is "home" or "abroad." Thus, you can say "I am going home," but if you want to say "my home" you must say "I am going to my home" and not "I am going my home."

You can say "I am going abroad," but not "I am going India." People often say "I wrote him" (which is wrong), when they mean "I wrote to him."

Where a verb is preceded by *to* the "infinitive" of the verb is formed, but this little matter will be discussed in Chapter IV.

INTERJECTIONS

The only remaining part of speech to be considered (apart from verbs and pronouns, which will be dealt with in the next two chapters) is the *interjection* or *exclamation*.

An exclamation such as "Ah!" or an exclamatory phrase such as "What nonsense!" plays no part in the construction of a sentence. It is a voluntary or involuntary remark, and as an exclamation it takes the exclamation mark (!), which will be considered in Chapter VII when the subject of punctuation is reached.

According to literature of a bygone age, and to pseudo-historical novels, our ancestors were in the habit of saying "Zounds!", "By Jove!" and "Gadzooks!". The commonest exclamations of the present day are perhaps "I say!", "Oh dear!", "Gracious!", "Indeed!", "Goodness!", "Alas!", "Good heavens!", "Gosh!", and the various expletives.

Quite often, "Alas!" is used parenthetically; that is, it can be put into a sentence in such a way that a break is formed. It can be an oratorical aid, as in: "The party's prospects—alas!—have been ruined by the irresponsible action of a few hotheads."

There is a curious exclamatory use of "Why!" which I cannot explain. "Why! He's done it again" is an example. Personally, I think it may be the sound of the word that so satisfactorily expresses surprise, or the shape of the mouth in saying it.

CHAPTER IV

Verbs

❖❖❖❖❖❖❖❖❖❖❖❖❖❖❖❖❖❖❖❖❖❖❖❖❖❖❖❖❖❖❖❖❖❖❖❖

Iᴛ is now time to say something else about verbs. As you know, verbs are the parts of speech which denote action, or "the doing of something." Thus, in the simple sentences, "I go," "He had," "She will come," "I shall leave," the verbs are *go, had, will come* and *shall leave*.

The meaning of tenses—past, present and future—is well enough known. In the above short sentences, *go* is in the present tense, *had* in the past tense, and both *will come* and *shall leave* are in the future tense. As this book is not primarily intended as an elementary treatise on English, I propose to deal in this chapter with a few features about verbs which are not so well known, or about which there may be doubt.

In one way, verbs are the most important of the parts of speech, for, as you will see in Chapter VI, a verb is an essential part of a true sentence.

MOODS

Sometimes in grammar you hear about *moods*, but this is simply a technical term and nothing to be afraid of. *Mood* is a corruption of *mode*, or form, and it would have been more explanatory if the word *mode* had been kept alive in this connection.

While there are three tenses of verbs—past, present and future —there are four verb moods. These are the infinitive, the conditional, the subjunctive and the imperative. There used to be a so-called indicative mood—the form of a verb implying affirmation, denial or questioning—but as it called for no special construction it has ceased to be recognised, and we shall waste no time on it.

One tense may have different moods, and we shall deal with each mood as we come to it.

THE INFINITIVE

I first mentioned the infinitive in a brief note on page 23. A verb written or said by itself, when applied to nothing in particular, is unlimited, or infinite, in scope, and thus we have the term *infinitive*.

"I work," "You work," "He works," "They work," are all particular applications of the act of working; but "to work" is the general function, unlimited in scope, and thus the infinitive mood of the verb. The use of the infinitive is necessary to complete certain kinds of statement, as in the following: "I am going to work," "He means to eat his breakfast," and "They hope to catch the train."

In talking or writing about verbs in general it is usual to give them infinitive forms. Thus we refer to the verbs *to eat, to live, to sleep, to open*. In languages other than English the preposition *to* is implied; thus, in French, the infinitive forms of the four verbs above are *manger* (to eat), *vivre* (to live), *dormir* (to sleep), and *ouvrir* (to open).

THE SPLIT INFINITIVE

The inclusion, or implication, of the little word *to* in the infinitives of other languages may be the origin of the dictum that in English it is shocking to "split" the infinitive—that is, to insert a word or words between *to* and its verb. Here are some examples of split infinitives:

"He started *to slowly walk* down the road."

"I want *to further examine* your proposals."

"He was forced *to unconsciously shield* his eyes from the glare."

"It would be better to ignore the letter than *to belatedly and clumsily proffer* your apologies."

One thing that strikes us about these sentences is their awkwardness. None of them *sounds* right. Here they are without the split infinitives:

"He started to walk slowly down the road."

"I want to examine your proposals further."

"He was unconsciously forced to shield his eyes from the glare."

"It would be better to ignore the letter than belatedly and clumsily proffer your apologies." (This sentence has been improved simply by the removal of *to*.)

Yet it is not entirely on grounds of euphony (smoothness or agreeability of sound) that infinitive-splitting is condemned. The most likely reason, as we have seen, is the fact that in most Western languages the infinitive form of a verb, being one word only, cannot be split.

Our own language is English, however, and I am with those who do not see why the rules of English grammar should be rigidly based on the rules of older or foreign grammars. I do not like splitting an infinitive, and I should not split an infinitive deliberately, but I have no patience with those pedants who howl in disdain if they catch anyone doing it, whatever the justification.

THE JUSTIFIED SPLIT INFINITIVE

Many good newspapers have a rule against the split infinitive, and "copy" containing a split infinitive is usually altered. There are times, however, when it is more melodious and less artificial to split an infinitive than to stick slavishly to the rule. Consider the following three sentences:

"We regret it is impossible to legally authorise the termination of the lease.

"We regret it is impossible to authorise legally the termination of the lease."

"We regret it is impossible legally to authorise the termination of the lease."

I think you will agree that the first is the smoothest and the third the roughest. The third, moreover, is ambiguous, since the adverb *legally* could be related to *is impossible*; that is, the sentence could mean "We regret it is legally impossible. . . ."

THE SPLIT INFINITIVE: CONCLUSIONS

The conclusions about the split infinitive, then, seem to be these.

Avoid it if you can. If you find that avoiding it makes the

sentence sound unnatural or ambiguous, split the infinitive. But preferably—and this is my own way of escape—remodel the sentence rather than split the infinitive.

OMISSION OF "TO" FROM THE INFINITIVE

There are legitimate cases where, in the use of an infinitive, the word *to* is understood but not expressed—that is, it is implied. An example is: "Help me bring in the coal."

The omission of *to* before *bring* is a very common example of "ellipsis" (a shortening), especially in conjunction with the verb *to help*. There is nothing wrong with this kind of sentence, and we shall say no more about it.

PRESENT-TENSE CONSTRUCTION

English is a language in which there is a present-tense construction like "I am waiting" for "I wait." Although the meaning of the two sentences is almost the same there is a subtle difference. "I am waiting" implies a somewhat prolonged wait, and "I wait" rather implies a short wait.

Perhaps a more suitable example to show the slight difference would be "I am shooting." This means that I am in the act of shooting—loading, getting into position, and firing—while "I shoot" could probably involve only the firing. "I shoot" could also mean that I customarily indulge in the sport of shooting, in which connection "I am shooting" would be clearly absurd.

It is in this general, imprecise sense, in fact, that the present-tense construction without *am* is nowadays nearly always used. "He writes" might mean anything. "He writes novels" signifies a current but not necessarily continuous habit of the person discussed. But "He is writing" means that he is writing at this moment, or at this particular time.

PAST-TENSE CONSTRUCTION

It will be concluded from the foregoing that in English there are two present-tense constructions, while in most other European languages there is only one.

There are two corresponding constructions in the past tense— "I waited" and "I was waiting." For "I was waiting" some other languages have an equivalent which the French call the "past-imperfect." The imperfect, I think, is a very suitable term, for the construction is more vague, less definite, than the equivalent of "I waited."

PARTICIPLES

Participles are those forms of a verb ending (for example) in -*ing* and -*ed*. Thus, in "I am waiting," *waiting* is the *present participle* of the verb "to wait," and in "I have waited" *waited* is the *past participle*.

Present participles invariably end in -*ing*. Past participles, on the other hand, have various endings, as in *known, been, gone, come, lost*, but the commonest ending is -*ed*. A participle is often used as a *verbal adjective*, as in "the rising sun" and "the lost pibroch."

The past participle *lost* is an example of a -*t* ending. Other -*t* endings are in *learnt, dreamt*, and *leapt*. It is true that these past participles are often interchanged with the simple past tense of the verbs—*learned, dreamed* and *leaped*—but I prefer to keep the -*t* endings for the past participles. Thus, I say "I dreamed" and "I have dreamt," the -*ed* ending, after all, being common to most other verbs in their past-tense constructions.

An unusual case of a dual form is provided by *past* and *passed*. Both are past participles of the verb "to pass," but while *past* is used with the verb "to be" *passed* is used with the verb "to have." The sentences "I am past middle age" and "I have passed middle age" are both correct.

PAST TENSE AND PAST PARTICIPLE

For a great many verbs the past tense is the same as the past participle, examples being: "I passed," "I have passed," "I loved," "I have loved," "He dug," "He has dug," "They read," "They have read."

Be on your guard, however, with the following verbs—the so-called "strong" verbs—in which the dominant vowel is *i*:—

Infinitive	*Past tense*	*Past participle*
to drink	drank	have (has) drunk
to sink	sank	have (has) sunk

to swim	swam	have (has) swum
to sing	sang	have (has) sung
to begin	began	have (has) begun

Far too often you hear the *a* vowel used instead of the *u* vowel and the *u* instead of the *a*.

VERBS ENDING IN "T" OR "D"

Verbs which can cause doubt include those ending in *t* or *d*, for example, *bet*, *let*, *hit*, *sit*, *bid*, *pad*, *rid* and *bud*.

I am afraid that the past-tense and past-participle forms of these verbs are maddeningly inconsistent, and the only guide to "correctness" is accepted usage.

With regard to *bet*, it is usual to say "I bet him five pounds" in a particular application, or "I have bet on a horse." Yet, when speaking of betting in a general sense, we say such things as "They betted all day long." These forms sound more pleasant than "I betted him five pounds" and "They bet all day long." If the second sentence is in the present tense, of course, it is the only way of saying it.

The past tense and past participle of *let*, on the other hand, are always *let*. It would never occur to anyone to say anything other than "I let my house" or "I have let my house," just as no one would think of saying "I hitted him" or "I have hitted him."

The past tense and past participle of *bid*, in the auction-room sense, are both *bid*, as in "I bid him ten pounds" or "I have bid him ten pounds." In the other sense of *bid*, however, the past tense is *bade* and the past participle *bidden*, as illustrated in the two sentences: "His mother bade him come home" and "She has bidden him not to go." (Observe the curious omission of *to* before *come* and its inclusion before *go*.)

Pad, unlike *bid*, always changes into *padded*. "The cat padded about the room while I padded the cushions." *Rid* is similar, as in the sentences: "The cat has ridded the house of mice" and "We ridded them of the unwelcome guest." It is, however, perfectly acceptable to say "I was well rid of him." The past tense and past participle of bud, nevertheless, are always *budded*.

I have not yet enlarged on the verb *sit* as it can do with a short section to itself.

THE VERB "TO SIT"

The past tense and past participle of *sit* can be *sat* or *seated*. Usage is strange, for the following examples of accepted English show no apparent rule or regularity:

"They all sat."

"I sat down."

"We have sat here long enough."

"I sat on the chair."

"I seated (sat) my baby on the stool."

"Are you all seated?"

"Pray be seated."

We often hear (for example) of a "deep-seated complaint." Strictly, the adverb *deeply* should be used, but common licence permits otherwise. The past participle *seated* is contained in the compound adjective, and *deep-sat* would sound odd.

"SHALL" AND "WILL"

There is much confusion over *shall* and *will* and their "conditional" forms *should* and *would*. Even people whose grammar is almost faultless in other respects fall down in the use of these words, and there is a common delusion that *shall* and *will*, or *should* and *would*, are interchangeable, that the difference between each pair is so slight as to be negligible.

The delusion is far from reality. Generally the fault is to use *will* for *shall* and *would* for *should*, rather than the reverse.

For plain future-tense construction—that is, mere statement of intention—it is correct to say "I shall" and "We shall." It is also correct to say "You will" and "They will."

"I shall go home." This is right if I am simply affirming my intention of going home in the future. Similarly, "You will go home" and "They will go home" are correct if future or almost-immediate actions are simply being stated.

"I will," or "We will," on the other hand, is not used for a plain statement of intention, but only when there is a choice, or volition (exercise of the will). If I say "I will go home" I mean that I have the choice of going or not going, that I really want to go home, that I have considered the possibility of not going home but discarded the idea.

Thousands of English-speaking people, however, use *I will*

simply as future tense, whatever the shade of meaning. I am not sure whether to class such people as illiterates, for many writers are merely careless in this respect.

CONDITIONAL FORMS

Later on I shall explain at length the term "conditional" as used in grammar, but, briefly, the words *should* and *would* are the conditional forms of *shall* and *will*.

Thus, if I said "I would go home," the true meaning would be that, given the *choice* of staying or going home, I should prefer to go home. But people spoil it by saying "I would like to go home," and this construction is wrong. If you want to use the word *like* you must say "I should like to go home," or if you want to use *prefer* you must say "I should prefer to go home."

Another legitimate use of *would* for the first person is in such constructions as the following:

"I *would* call and find nobody in."

"We *would* decide to go for a picnic when it's raining." In such cases *would* is usually emphasised, the implication being that it is the subject's misfortune to have made a wrong choice.

Should, of course, can also and very commonly mean "ought to," or "am [is, are] obliged to," but this use has no place in our present study.

GENERAL RULES FOR "SHALL," "WILL," "SHOULD" AND "WOULD"

The first person *I* or *we*, for plain future-tense or conditional construction, takes *shall* or *should*.

The following examples of the use of *will*, however, can be either right or wrong:

"I will give up my seat to the lady."

"We will proceed to the next stage of the negotiations." If there is any argument about giving up the seat, *will* is right. If the sentence is purely a statement of intention, *will* should be *shall*. If there is a choice between proceeding and not proceeding, *will* is right. If the speaker is merely telling his listeners what is going to happen next, *will* is wrong and should be changed to *shall*.

The following examples are wrong:

"I would prefer not to answer."

"If the town was besieged we would still have enough to eat."

You may argue that in the first example of those two there is a choice between answering and not answering, and that *would* is therefore justified. But the verb related to *would* is *prefer*, a definite action. You could say here, correctly, either "I will answer" or "I will not answer." If you want to use the word *prefer*, however, you must say "I should prefer not to answer."

For plain future-tense or conditional construction, the second person (*you*) and the third person (*he, she, they* or a pronoun) take *will* or *would*. The usual practice is correct, except in parts of the English Midlands (Nottingham, for example), where very many people have developed the atrocious habit of saying "Shall you do it?"

The abbreviations *I'll, you'll, he'll, she'll, we'll* and *they'll* cover both *shall* and *will*. In speech and written dialogue, therefore, these abbreviations are nicely convenient.

SOME QUOTATIONS

Many writers, I said a little earlier, are merely careless in the use or misuse of *will*. Defaulters may comfort themselves with the reflection that they are not necessarily always in bad company.

In the following lines from respected poets there is no implication of choice:

"I will arise and go now, and go to Innisfree." (W. B. Yeats.)

"I will make you brooches, and toys for your delight," (Robert Louis Stevenson.)

In a line from Robert Bridges, "I will not let thee go," the poet is correct as there is an apparent choice between letting-go and not letting-go.

The tremendous statement in the Marriage Service, "I will," is also correct. "I shall" would not be nearly strong enough, for the vows are much more than mere statements of intentions, and indicate a choice of action after serious consideration.

INDEFINITE FUTURE WITH "SHALL"

If a future action is indefinite, or only casually hinted at, or used vaguely in an idiomatic manner, *shall* is customary not only for the first person but also for the second and third.

The following examples illustrate my meaning:

"When the nation has no more use for him, he shall be cast into the wilderness."

"John shall always be the first to arrive." (But the *definite* future would be: "John will be the first to arrive tomorrow.")

"Perhaps some time there shall be world peace."

"Virtue shall not go unrewarded."

"Nation shall rise against nation."

I admit that in a great many such sentences as these the use of *will* instead of *shall* goes unnoticed, and there are innumerable borderline cases where either word would be justified.

"SHALL" WITH "THAT"-CLAUSES

We often use the word *that* after clauses incorporating such verbs as *demand, be anxious* and *intend*. Future tense in most cases of this kind is expressed by *shall*, as in the following:

"The chairman demands that every member shall be in his place by seven o'clock."

"We are anxious that this special concession shall be extended to all applicants."

"The Government intends that all such persons shall benefit by this order." (This would be better expressed as: "The Government intends all such persons to benefit. . . .")

The pronoun *I*, of course, takes *shall* naturally in such cases.

"WILL" WITH "THAT"-CLAUSES

That-clauses taking *will* are those incorporating, for example, *hope, fear* and *anticipate*, where the outcome is indefinite. Examples are:

"It is hoped that many members of the company will be present."

"If he went out in this storm I fear that he would get lost." (This is an example of the conditional.)

"It is a difficult climb, and we do not anticipate that he will reach the summit."

Again, of course, the pronoun *I* naturally takes *shall*, as in "I hope that I shall pass my examination."

In some cases the word *that* can be omitted, but in the omission you should be sparing. Thus, although the second and third of the above examples could be read quite smoothly without *that*, the first would sound incomplete. This point will be discussed further in Chapter V (page 63).

"EXPECT"

It is not usual to adopt *shall* or *will* in a construction with *expect*. Normal constructions are, for example, the following:

"England expects every man to do his duty."

"I expect it to be fine tomorrow."

"They expect to be well treated."

If we wish to use *shall* or *will*, however, we should remember that the verb *expect* takes *shall* only if the expectation is strict. or peremptory. *Shall* would thus be applied only in the first of these examples:

"England expects that every man shall do his duty."

"I expect that it will be fine tomorrow."

"They expect that they will be well treated."

I shall remind you again that the pronoun *I* takes *shall*, as in "I expect that I shall be late."

THE CONDITIONAL

Several times in the preceding pages we have referred to "the conditional." The conditional is not a tense but a mood, and whereas in French, for example, there is a special form of verb for the conditional, in English it is expressed by the addition of *should*, *would* or *could* to the verb.

Simple examples are:

"If you came home you would be welcomed."

"If I said such a thing I should be ashamed."

"He could do the job if he had the tools."

Thus, very often (but not always), the conditional is accompanied by an *if*-clause, stating the condition. In the three sentences just given, the conditions are:

"*If* you came home . . ."
"*If* I said such a thing . . ."
"*If* he had the tools . . ."

It will have been noticed that, when used conditionally, *if* takes the past tense – *came* (not *come*), *said* (not *say*), *had* (not *has*).

REDUNDANT CONDITIONALS

So much is self-evident. The thing to avoid, however, and which is not so self-evident, is the clumsy construction with a redundant conditional and past participle.

Often you hear this kind of thing:

"I should have thought that it would have been necessary to inform the people."

If the speaker says, correctly, "It would have been necessary to inform the people," that is one thing. If he says, also correctly, "I should have thought," that is another thing.

But the compound statement requires only one conditional and one past participle to give the meaning. The speaker's opinion could be correctly expressed in one of two ways, *either:*

"I should have thought that it was necessary to inform the people," or "I think it would have been necessary to inform the people." (The second sentence sounds better with *that* omitted.)

THE SUBJUNCTIVE

In Chapter III I mentioned "the subjunctive." The subjunctive is a mood which, in English, is almost obsolete, but is still perfectly legitimate when used in the right place. In French it is still very much alive, like the conditional.

The subjunctive is the form of a verb used for something that might have been imagined but did not actually occur; for a hypothesis, but not for a fact. In modern practice the effect of its use is confined to the verb *to be.*

A common living example of a subjunctive is "If I were you . . ." *I* could never be *you*; therefore the use of the subjunctive *were* is legitimate.

In most *if*-sentences or clauses the subjunctive can safely be used as long as the sentence is not concerned with fact or with likely possibility. Thus, another correct example of its use is: "If I were given wings I should fly away."

In a bygone age we could have used constructions like (for instance) "If his theory be correct . . ." (instead of "is correct"). His theory might be correct. We may even know it is correct, and choose to start our sentence in an oratorical way. Hence it may *not* be mere assumption, or hypothesis, that his theory is correct, and it would be preferable by modern standards to use *is*.

In general, the only subjunctive now used with *if* is *were* and not *be*, except perhaps in poetry and fanciful oratory. One construction, with an understood *if* omitted, has lasted since Gay's *The Beggar's Opera* (1727):

> "How happy could I be with either,
> Were t'other dear charmer away!"

This type of sentence is in common use to-day; for example: "Were I to go home I might find it" instead of "If I should go home . . ."

A recognised modern use of *be* is in such constructions as: "Though he be hale and hearty, he cannot sleep."

A further surviving use of the subjunctive is with "I wish . . .," as in: "I wish the examination were over."

The subjunctive is also used as a conditional, as in: "It were more seemly if you appeared," instead of "It would be more seemly if you appeared."

THE SUBJUNCTIVE: SUMMARY

Use a subjunctive *were* with *if* when dealing with a hypothetical or imaginary situation.

Use a subjunctive *were* with *if* in an "I wish. . . ." construction.

Use a subjunctive *were* in a hypothetical or actual situation if the *if* is omitted.

Use a subjunctive *be* with *though* or *although*.

Refrain from using a subjunctive *be* if the result sounds artificial or stilted.

Subjunctive conditionals are permissible.

Use the subjunctive mood sparingly, and only if you are sure you are using it correctly.

THE IMPERATIVE

The word *imperative* denotes urgency, anxiety, as in: "It is absolutely imperative that we catch the night train." It denies the existence of any choice or alternative.

From there it is easy to see how the imperative mood arose. Commands and orders are given in the imperative mood of a verb. "Come!" "Go!" "Take it away!" "Halt!" All these are examples of the imperative. Usually an imperative word or clause is followed by an exclamation mark, this being one of the few cases where an exclamation mark is justified.

Other examples of the imperative are:

"Politics be blowed!" (This is an abbreviation of "Let politics be blowed!"

"Out of my way!" ("Get" is understood.)

"Let the earth be filled with the fruits of Thy goodness." (An imperative sentence of some length may not need the exclamation mark.)

"Cry 'Havoc!', and let slip the dogs of war."

TRANSITIVE AND INTRANSITIVE VERBS

"I hammer the nail."

"I sleep in peace."

What is the difference between the two verbs *hammer* and *sleep*?

Briefly, the difference is that you can hammer something, but you cannot sleep something. *Sleep*, as a verb, is sufficient in itself.

The word "transitive," like all those other "trans-" words, is derived from the Latin prefix meaning "across," "over," "beyond" or "through," and a transitive verb is one which directly connects the *subject* of a sentence with its *object*. We are rather anticipating the material of Chapter VI, but it does not matter. If the subject can do something with the verb to the object, the verb is transitive.

Transitive verbs that suggest themselves are "hit," "eat," "read," "spend," "take," "repair," "write," "organise" and "simplify." Most transitive verbs can at times be used without an object.

An intransitive verb, as I have pointed out, can exist by

itself, without an object. Thus the simple sentence "I live" makes sense as it stands. An intransitive verb can, however, connect the object with the subject through a preposition or through a phrase. "I live" can be expanded into "I live in my house" (through the preposition *in*) or into "I live very close to a stream" (through the phrase *very close to*).

"LAY" AND "LIE"

Discussion of transitive and intransitive verbs gives a golden opportunity to discuss the often ill-treated verbs *to lay* and *to lie*.

To lay is transitive. That is, you can lay something down. You can lay a book on a table, and a hen can lay an egg.

To lie is intransitive—not only in the sense of telling an untruth, but also in the sense of "to recline," which is our concern here.

Lie is sufficient in itself, as in the following:

"I lie on the bed."

"The dog lies on the floor."

"She went to lie down."

These are all correct examples of the use of the verb *to lie*.

Most people are fairly well conversant with the difference between *lay* and *lie*, but illiterate and semi-literate people very often use *lay* when they mean *lie*. They say, for instance:

"I was laying down when the butcher called."

"My grandmother went for a lay-down."

"LAY" AND "LIE": PAST TENSE

The origin of the above error—the use of *lay* instead of *lie*—is no doubt due to the fact that the past tense of *lie* is *lay*, as in:

"I lay on the bed."

"The dog lay on the floor."

"She went to lie down" is still correct, for the past tense of the sentence is conveyed by the verb *went*.

The past tense of *lay*, on the other hand, is *laid*, as in:

"I laid the book on the table."

"The hen laid an egg."

"LAY" AND "LIE": PAST PARTICIPLES

So far, so good. But the difficulties to some people seem to increase when past participles are involved.

The following are correct examples of the use of the past participles.

To lay "I have laid the book on the table."

   "The hen has laid an egg."

To lie "I have lain on the bed."

   "The dog has lain on the floor."

It is important to remember that *lain* is *NEVER* used with the verb *to lay*, and *laid* is *NEVER* used with the verb *to lie*.

"LAY" AND "LIE": COMPOUND VERBS

Some people get themselves more and more involved, even in print, when they start dealing with the compound verbs *overlay*, *underlay*, *overlie* and *underlie*. Frequently sentences like the following are heard or read:

"The sandstones are overlaid by the shales."

"The case was underlaid by the secret that they were twins."

"Having overlain the primer by the first undercoating, allow to dry thoroughly."

"The author then became convinced that the low-grade ore overlaid the old workings."

The first three sentences are examples of the wrong past participle, and the fourth sentence (by a supposedly educated scientist) is an example of the use of the wrong word for the past tense.

If in doubt about the correct form, first ask yourself your meaning. The meanings of the above sentences are:

"The shales *overlie* the sandstones."

"The secret that they were twins *underlay* the case."

"Having *laid* the first undercoating over the primer, allow it to dry thoroughly."

". . . . the low-grade ore *lay* over the old workings." Now, you know that the past participle of *lay* is *laid* and the past participle of *lie* is *lain*. Then the first three sentences, corrected, should be:

"The sandstones are overlain by the shales."

"The case was underlain by the secret that they were twins."

"Having overlaid the primer . . ."

And you know that the past tense of *lie* is *lay*, so that the fourth sentence should be:

"The author then became convinced that the low-grade ore overlay the old workings."

THE VERB "TO BE"

There are a few anomalies (irregularities), and some special features, to be observed about the verb *to be*. These will be described under separate headings.

THE COMPLEMENT

Where the verb *to be* is accompanied by a pronoun forming the object of a sentence or clause—the "complement" of the verb—the pronoun must be subjective. (Subject and object are to be discussed in Chapter VI.)

Examples

Wrong	Right
"This is him [her]."	"This is he [she]."
"It was me."	"It was I."
"I am him [her]."	"I am he [she]."
"The people you saw were us."	"The people you saw were we."
"Those are them."	"Those are they."

The fact that this rule is often broken in conversation is no excuse for breaking it in writing, unless dialogue is being quoted.

VARIATION IN NUMBERS

The subject of a sentence may differ *in number* from its object; that is, one may be singular when the other is plural.

The verb, then, takes the number of the subject, as in:

"My wages *are* one pound."

"One pound *is* my wages."

"The actions of the enemy *were* a blot on civilisation."

"These pages *are* the part to be omitted."

"The part to be omitted *is* these pages."

"Consols *are* a sound speculation."

"A sound speculation *is* Consols."

"Examinations *are* a necessary evil."

COMPOUND SUBJECTS

By a compound subject I mean a subject *compounded* of two or more words of which, for our present purposes, one is singular and the other plural, as in "One of these things."

The verb *to be* in this case takes the singular form. A correct example is: "One of these eggs *is* bad." Occasionally, however, you hear the wrong construction: "One of these eggs *are* bad."

"AM I NOT?"

We can say, perfectly correctly, "I'm not," but unfortunately there is no recognised abbreviation for "Am I not?" We can say "Haven't I?", "Aren't we?", "Hasn't he?" and "Isn't she?" But when we want to abbreviate "Am I not?" we realise we cannot do it easily.

At one time "Ain't I?" was recognised in polite conversation, and it is a pity that it is now only used by some of the uneducated. "Aren't I?" is quite common, but is so obviously wrong that it invites shudders.

There is a great deal to be said for the usage, often heard amongst Scots, of "Amn't I?", and I see nothing against its introduction into standard English. At least it is perfectly grammatical. If you do not like it, however—possibly because of the awkwardness of the sudden switch from *m* to *n*—I am afraid you will have to be content with "Am I not?"

ELLIPSIS WITH "TO BE" AND "TO HAVE"

Ellipsis means "a shortening," and although in grammar it takes several forms I shall concern myself here only with its effects on the verbs *to be* and *to have*.

Instead of saying "He was leading and I was following," we could say "He was leading and I following." The omission of the second *was* constitutes an example of ellipsis, as it is "understood" to be covered by the first *was*.

So much is clear, and such ellipsis forms part of everyday writing and speech.

It is often thought that where one of the subjects is singular and the other plural, each verb must take its appropriate case, as in: "They were leading and I was following." There is nothing wrong with this, but in short sentences, where the two subjects are close together—in this case, *They* and *I*—it is permissible to omit the second verb. The sentence would then become: "They were leading and I following."

Other permissible examples are:

"You are fifty and I sixty."

"He has an umbrella and I a raincoat."

IMPERMISSIBLE ELLIPSIS

In the examples given, the two subjects are comparable; each statement would still make sense if the subjects were interchanged. But if the subjects are not comparable, ellipsis of this kind is not permissible.

For instance, consider the sentence: "The road was long and they hungry."

With the subjects interchanged the sentence does not make sense; obviously the road could not be hungry, and the subjects are therefore not comparable. The sentence should read, then: "The road was long and they were hungry."

Where the two subjects are some distance removed from each other the practice is not to be tolerated. Think of the clumsiness of the following: "They were leading, and I, who had just come out of hospital and was feeling weak, following."

By the time the reader has reached the word *weak* he has mentally lost touch with the start of the sentence and the subject *I*. There is clearly something lacking; and all that is necessary is the insertion of *was* before *following*.

CHAPTER V

Pronouns

◆◆◆◆◆◆◆◆◆◆◆◆◆◆◆◆◆◆◆◆◆◆◆◆◆◆◆◆◆◆◆◆◆◆◆◆◆◆

A great deal could be written about pronouns, for of all the parts of speech they are perhaps the most loosely used. Strictly, a pronoun is a word taking the place of a noun which has already been referred to or is understood, but many words which for the sake of convenience are called pronouns do not easily fall into this definition.

Pronouns are sometimes classified, accepted classifications being, for example, personal pronouns, demonstrative pronouns, relative pronouns and interrogative pronouns. Some pronouns can belong to more than one kind, and this is one reason why classifications should not be studied too rigidly. The classifications are convenient for description, however, and will be followed here, but as long as you know a pronoun when you hear or see one it matters little what sort of pronoun it is.

PERSONAL PRONOUNS

Personal pronouns—the easiest to recognise—can take the place of proper names or of articled nouns like *the man*.

In the next chapter I am to explain the differences between *subject* and *object*. For the present all I shall say is that the subjective and objective forms of the personal pronouns are the following:—

Subject	Object		Subject	Object
I	Me		We	Us
He	Him		You	You
She	Her		They	Them

Examples of the use of personal pronouns are unnecessary, but examples of their abuse are found so frequently, and are so common, that they will receive special attention later in the book.

"YOU"

An idiomatic use of *you*, similar in application to the French *on*, is its substitution for *one* or *anyone*. As this use of *you* often sounds less pedantic than *one*, it has become accepted English, especially in conversation.

In writing, however—unless in the writing of quoted speech—its use must be carefully controlled. Over-liberal use of *you* for *one* can dangerously approach slovenliness.

Care must be taken, also, not to use both *you* and *one* in the same sentence or in the same passage. One of the drawbacks of *you* is that once one starts applying the idiom one cannot change over to *one* until a decent interval has elapsed.

DEMONSTRATIVE PRONOUNS

Demonstrative pronouns, as is fairly obvious, have the duty of demonstrating, as in the following sentences:—

"*This* is my apple."

"*That* is her peach."

"*These* are your pears."

"*Those* are his plums."

The personal pronoun *they* can also be demonstrative, as in

"*They* are the people I like."

In each of the above sentences the demonstrative pronoun (printed in *italics*) is the subject. The objective forms of the words, however (except for *they*) are the same, as in:—

"I want *this*."

"You want *that*."

"He wants *these*."

"She wants *those*."

In the case of *they*, the objective form is the same as the subjective form only if the verb is the verb "to be." Thus, "Those are *they*" is correct, and "Those are *them*" is wrong.

The use of *them* as object is correct for all other verbs, as in "I have *them*" and "You ate *them*."

Them is often ignorantly used as subject, and we commonly hear sentences such as "Them are the ones I like," or even

"Them is . . . ." During the war foreign Servicemen were liable to learn peculiar kinds of English, and in one city in East Scotland a good-hearted local girl, piloting a Polish soldier through the intricacies of shopping, pointed to a box of apples and carefully explained: "Them's aipples."

DEMONSTRATIVE PRONOUNS IN USE

When we use demonstrative pronouns our reader or listener must know what we are referring to. Apart from the simple examples already given, further examples, of a type very widely used, are the following:—

"This drawing supersedes *that* dated August, 19..."

"Employees to whom it applies are *those* with green cards."

Besides *this, that, these* and *those*, however, there are other pronouns which deserve to be included in the demonstrative class. These are:—

None	Neither	Some
All	Either	Any

DEMONSTRATIVE PRONOUNS AS ADJECTIVES

Except for *none,* demonstrative pronouns can be used as adjectives before nouns, as secondary adjectives before adjectives and nouns, and as adjectives in the form of articles. The subjective and objective forms are the same, examples being:—

"I adore those roses."

"These foolish things remind me of you."

"Please give me this at."

"That happy man hasn't a care in the world."

The use of demonstrative pronouns as adjectives with the word *one*—as in "this one" and, very colloquially, "these ones"— is unjustified, as the word "ones" is quite superfluous. Incidentally, the use of "one" in this sense makes it a pronoun.

Consider the sentence: "These apples are good, but those are better." *These* is an adjective describing the apples. *Those* can be either a demonstrative pronoun demonstrating which apples are referred to, or an abbreviation of "those apples", but, as the result is the same whichever way you look at it, it does not matter.

What *does* matter, however, is how you refer to kinds of things. You must never say "those kind" of anything. Say "those kinds," if you like, or "these kinds" or "this kind" or "that kind." But to say "those kind" is to apply a plural adjective to a singular noun. This crime, though indefensible, is on the increase among writers and public speakers.

"NONE"

The word *none* sometimes presents difficulties in the choice of the appropriate verb form. Should we say "None is" or "None are," "None come" or "None comes"?

If we have been taught that *none* is always singular, then obviously, in our own estimation, "None is" and "None comes" are correct. But there are no reasonable grounds for assuming that *none* is always singular, and the word can have a plural application, in which case "None are" and "None come" are correct.

My advice in deciding whether to say "None is" or "None are" is to consider the context, consider the sense, consider the sound, and then make up your mind. You need not be ashamed of saying "None are" if the sense of the sentence supports it and it *sounds* right, as in "None are coming tonight."

"EITHER" AND "NEITHER"

It is surprising, indeed astonishing, that while *either* is usually applied correctly, *neither* causes much fumbling and downright hideousness of grammar even among the "best" authors and the more responsible newspapers.

"Either solution is correct" comes easily to most people. But every day we read sentences like "Neither Dickens nor Thackeray were panderers to the public taste" instead of "Neither Dickens nor Thackeray was a panderer to the public taste."

Either and *neither* are very logical words, and the rule of application is simple. You know already, of course, that *either* is used with *or* and *neither* is used with *nor*, and as *neither* seems to cause the more confusion in the public mind I shall confine my remarks to this word.

If both the things under discussion are singular, *neither* takes the singular number of its following verb, as in: "Neither General A. nor General B. can be considered a first-class strategist."

You can say "neither are" only if both things spoken about are plural, as in: "Neither men nor women are eligible," and "Neither birds nor fish are mammals." Although it is as elementary as that, *neither* leads to much abuse, and I shall have more to say about it in Chapter IX.

Difficulty arises when one of the things you are dealing with takes the singular form of the verb and the other, the plural. What should be said in the following cases?

"Neither you nor I was [were] there."

"Although it was a vine harvest, neither grapes nor wine were [was] much in abundance."

There is no solution to this difficulty, and the wise course is to evade the dilemma by a different construction. Personally, if faced with the above two examples, I should say:

"Neither of us was there" or "You and I weren't there."

"Although it was a vine harvest, there were not many grapes and there was little wine."

Sometimes you will hear *neither* applied to more than two things, or sets of things, as in: "Neither men nor women nor children were allowed to leave." This is as wrong as: "Either men or women or children . . ." but for some obscure reason the second sort of construction (with *either*) is seldom heard.

"EITHER" AND "NEITHER" WITH OTHER PARTS OF SPEECH

Either and *neither* can also, of course, be used with other parts of speech besides nouns, but they are then no longer pronouns.

With verb	"He can either come or go."
	"I could neither laugh nor cry."
With adverb	"Do it either willingly or unwillingly."
	"She wrapped it up neither neatly nor carefully."
With adjective	"I will have either red or blue paint."
	"She was neither beautiful nor ugly."
With preposition	"It is a long way either to or from school."
	"He took it neither by nor with your leave."

"ALL"

Though the useful little word *all* is also an adjective, I include it among the pronouns by virtue of its use in such constructions as:

"He left all to his son."

"Of the hundred candidates, all passed."

As an adjective of number, *all* takes a plural, as in "all men" or "all the men," and as in Orwell's classic dictum: "All animals are equal, but some animals are more equal than others."

All can be singular in a limited sense, as in "I ate all the jam," where jam is something that can be divided, or in "Do you want all the table?" In these cases, however, *all* probably means "all the parts of," so that it might be regarded as a plural after all.

"After all." What does that mean? This is one of the innumerable idioms of our language, although it is interesting to note that the French similarly say "Après tout." In effect, it is simply an abbreviation of "After all the evidence has been considered," or "After all is said and done."

Often you come across "all of" instead of just "all." The word *of* is unnecessary, except in "all of it" and "all of them."

"SOME"

We often use constructions like: "Some man or other said . . ." and "He gave it to some urchin in the street."

The word *some* here signifies that we do not know which man or which urchin was involved. If we said "The man . . ." or ". . . . to the urchin," our listener or reader would know at once which man or which urchin was meant.

To say "A man . . ." or ". . . . to an urchin" could mean that the listener might or might not know the man or the urchin. But the use of *some* in this sense shows definitely that the speaker is ignorant of the identities. The same application is found in *somebody* and *someone*.

Some is also used as an adjective of indefinite number, examples being "You can trust some people," "I dislike some colours."

It can also mean "a portion" as opposed to "all," as in "some of them," "some of it." But here *of* is necessary in all cases. Thus, while we say "all the time" and "all the meat."

the corresponding constructions with *some* are "some of the time" and "some of the meat."

There is also the idiomatic, colloquial, exclamatory use of *some*. When Hitler spoke of wringing Britain's neck like that of a chicken, Churchill remarked: "Some chicken; some neck!"

RELATIVE PRONOUNS

"This is the boy *who* gave it to me."

"The pen, *which* I laid on the desk, is missing."

"You cannot bite the hand *that* feeds you."

"The ladies, *whose* clothes were most fashionable, gathered in the ante-room."

"I carefully examined the building, *of which* the foundations appeared solid."

"The person *who* was on the stairs was a visitor."

"The person *whom* I saw on the stairs was a visitor."

In the above sentences, the words in italics are called *relative pronouns*, as each connects a noun to a clause (or statement) to which it is related.

RELATIVE PRONOUNS WITH OTHER PRONOUNS

The relative pronouns can be related not only to nouns but also to other pronouns. The following are examples:

"I, who am old . . ."

"Give it to him who needs it most."

"That which is wrong is useless."

"I'll have any that fits."

"WHO" AND "WHOM"

Whom is the objective form of *who*, and both are applied *only* to personal nouns and pronouns. I shall not enlarge upon subject and object until the next chapter, and for the present shall confine my remarks to pointing out that you must not say such things as "The person who I saw . . ." or "Whom is the next speaker?"

Who and *whom* can cause confusion. In its simplest applications, however, the subjective use of *who* is usually clearly understood, as in such sentences as:

"I saw the man who did it."

"The lady who dealt with the enquiry is out of the office." In these sentences there is no room for confusion of thought, as there often is with the use of *whom*, further consideration of which will be deferred till Chapter IX.

Occasionally you may see *who* and *whom* applied to animals: "The horse who won the St. Leger . . . ," "The dog whom I entered at Cruft's . . . " In spite of their being living creatures, nevertheless, animals take the relative pronouns *which* and *that*.

"WHOSE"

The relative personal pronoun of possession is *whose*, the correct application of which is usually understood, as in the following:

"Only people whose homes are in danger appreciate domestic security to the full."

"James, whose father was a poet, concentrated on essays."

Time and time again you will come across *whose* applied to inanimate things. This practice is defended on the grounds of its "flexibility," but personally I dislike it. *Whose* should be as personal as *who* and *whom*. Here is an extract from a dramatic criticism in a leading daily newspaper:

"He has done it again at the Duchess, in a play whose full title is . . ." I should prefer: ". . . . in a play of which the full title is . . ." If readers see respectable writers committing errors of this kind, they can be forgiven for following the bad example.

"WHICH" AND "THAT"

There is no difference between *which* and *that* in their use as relative pronouns. "The stone which the builders refused . . ." can just as well be expressed: "The stone that the builders refused . . ."

Consider the two following sentences:

"The apple which I gave you is bad."

"The apple that I gave you is bad."

Both mean the same, but personally I prefer the first simply because it sounds slightly more musical. The choice between *which* and *that*, in fact, is influenced solely by the arrangement of the vowel sounds and consonants.

"The hat that I wore at the party" sounds better, in my opinion, than "The hat which I wore at the party."

In this example, however, and in the previous one, the relative pronoun could be omitted altogether, thus:

"The apple I gave you is bad."

"The hat I wore at the party . . ."

The relative pronoun can only be omitted in cases where it can be sufficiently "understood."

OMISSION OF THE RELATIVE PRONOUN

The omission of the relative pronoun, in cases where the sentence is still left intelligible, is one of those practices in English which can be accepted or rejected only by consideration of the "sound" of the particular passage.

But it *is* important that the sentence be left intelligible by the omission. In the preceding paragraph, for instance, the relative pronoun *which* could not possibly have been omitted.

The relative pronoun to be omitted sometimes carries a supporting verb, and this, too, is likewise discarded. In the following passage the relative pronouns and the supporting verbs which *could* be omitted are in square brackets.

"The conference, [which is] held at Scarborough every summer, is a representative gathering of all the provincial institutes in the country. It is refreshing to see these hundreds of young people, who have all given up their holidays and [who] have journeyed here at their own expense, joining together in a single common cause that has been justly described as 'ennobling.' The healthy tan [which has been] given by the sun, the cool grace [which] their outlook has bred in them, and the individual freedom of thought that distinguishes them from members of rival organisations, make you feel that the future of our race is assured."

Do not pay any attention to the sense of the passage, which is one of those empty pieces of prose it is easy to write. Whether or not the words in square brackets are included is a matter of personal judgment. On the whole, economy in words is to be encouraged as long as the language is not debased, and frequently such economy results in power and smoothness of rhythm. But if on reading over the passage you are convinced that the inclusion of a *who* or *which* or *that*, with a supporting verb if necessary, would improve the harmony, clarify the meaning, or remove any ambiguity, then you should certainly include it.

"WHICH" WITH A NOUN

Sometimes for the sake of emphasis the word *which*, when used as a relative pronoun, is followed by its related noun. "He was married in 1914, which year he was always to remember for other reasons, too."

The inclusion of the noun *year* after *which* clearly indicates the relationship between "1914" and the rest of the sentence. If you try to read or say the sentence without *year*, it sounds strangely incomplete.

Other examples are:

"Geoffrey Dawson was an editor of *The Times*, which paper had been founded in 1788."

"As the author of *Peter Pan*, which play was to have a phenomenal success, Barrie was unduly modest."

"THAT" RELATED TO A VERB

From a discussion of *which* and *that* in their capacity as relative pronouns, it is but a short step to the use of *that* when related to a verb.

In very common use are the phrases "confirm that," "believe that," "learn that," "understand that," "report that," and many others like them. Where the word *that* is understood it can occasionally be omitted, as in: "I believe you have a room vacant."

Of recent years, however, I have been dismayed to find a decadent tendency towards the omission of *that* far too often. The result usually sounds unbalanced and unformed, and such constructions as the following are heard and seen every day:

"Our customers report they are satisfied with our service in every way."

"Will you please confirm the man left of his own accord?"

"We learn the applicant had been a convict."

"Our correspondent understands the majority of the strikers have returned to work."

INTERROGATIVE PRONOUNS

Interrogative pronouns are those which interrogate, or ask questions.

"Who is that?"

"Which is the right road?"

"What did he say?"

In these sentences, *who*, *which* and *what* are the interrogative pronouns. *Whose*, which I have already mentioned as a personal possessive pronoun, can also be an interrogative pronoun, as in: "Whose are those?"

Which and *what*, like the demonstratives, can be used before nouns or before adjectives and nouns, examples being:

"Which road is the right one?"

"What man is that?"

For practical purposes, the two words *in this application* are sometimes interchangeable.

Thus, we could say: "What is the right road?" Usually, however, the question "Which . . . ?" signifies a choice from a definite number, and "What . . . ?" signifies a vague decision from an indefinite number. Illustrations are:

"Of these games, which would you like to play?"

"What would you like to play?"

Except in cases like those given, *what* can never be used for *which*. We still have more to say about *what*, however, in the next section.

"WHAT"

What is one of those many useful words in the English language which have several functions. As we have seen, it is an interrogative pronoun. It is also vulgarly used as a relative pronoun by the illiterate in place of *which*, *that* and *who* ("That man what you saw"), but we shall not waste time on this execrable practice.

What is now generally accepted as *that which*, and although I remember schoolmaster pedants who were opposed to it there seems to be nothing illegitimate in this custom. "What I do is my own business." This sounds better than: "That which I do is my own business."

Less gracious examples of this use of *what* are:

"He gave him what is called a knock-out."

"I made what was for me a big mistake."

You hear constructions like these every day. They are not very elegant, and are unnecessarily long. Both statements could be expressed more briefly and in better English.

The question "What?" is short for "What did you say?" While grammar is largely inflexible, social fashions in language change. Thirty or forty years ago a blunt "What?" in polite speech might have been looked upon as bad manners, but today it is usually preferred to "Pardon" or "Beg pardon," both of which, of course, are short for the much more pleasant "I beg your pardon."

In the sentence "I'll tell you what," the word *what* is the prelude to something that is vaguely understood. Thus, the sentence in full might be "I'll tell you what will happen," or "I'll tell you what we'll do." In this connection, of course, *what* means "that which."

There is also "What for?" meaning "Why?" Here, however, the body of the sentence, although omitted, is understood between the speaker and the addressed. It might be: "What did you hit him for?" or "What did she go for?" These two questions could follow "I hit him" and "She went."

The old idiom "Give him what-for" seems to have grown in use merely by constant repetition between one person and another. I have been unable to trace its origin.

POSSESSIVE PRONOUNS

Possessive pronouns are of two kinds—those used as adjectives, and those used alone.

Of the first kind, examples are *my*, *thy*, *his*, *her*, *its*, *our*, *your*, and *their*. Such words (except *his*) must be followed by nouns or by words or phrases acting as nouns, as in "My goings-out and comings-in." I do not think any more need be said about this kind of possessive pronoun, but I might point out that I have included the old-fashioned *thy* because (with *thou*) it is still part of the language.

Care must be taken not to put an apostrophe-*s* in the possessive *its*, and the reader is referred to my note on page 69.

The second kind of possessive pronoun comprises *mine*, *thine*, *his*, *hers*, *ours*, *yours* and *theirs*. These words are sometimes called "absolute" possessives as they can stand alone, examples being:

"This hat is mine."

"Those books are theirs."

"Was it hers?"

There is no apostrophe in the *s*-endings of these words, but occasionally you will see an apostrophe so misused. *Either* and *neither*, however, both have possessive forms, and both take the apostrophe (*either's*, *neither's*).

Formerly *mine* and *thine* were used for *my* and *thy* before vowels and the aspirate *h*. This was a pleasant practice, and it is a pity it has fallen into disuse. The translators of the Bible were capable exponents of it; consider, for example, such poetical prose as this:

"I will lift up mine eyes unto the hills, from whence cometh my help."

"So that thou incline thine ear unto wisdom, and apply thine heart to understanding . . . ."

"Rejoice not when thine enemy falleth, and let not thine heart be glad when he stumbleth."

Shakespeare, too, followed the adjectival use of *mine* and *thine*:

"Bid me discourse, I will enchant thine ear . . . "

". . . . he furnished me

From mine own library with volumes that

I prize above my dukedom."

"Shall I not take mine ease in mine inn but I shall have my pocket picked?"

INDEFINITE PRONOUNS

Some pronouns cannot easily be classified as personal, demonstrative, relative, interrogative or possessive.

If a pronoun cannot be put neatly into any of these pigeonholes, and yet is unmistakably a pronoun, it can be labelled an *indefinite* pronoun. This term is also applied to a pronoun if there is doubt or vagueness about the noun for which it is substituted.

Some of the pronouns which we have already discussed are in some ways indefinite pronouns, but if they deserve classifications I feel they should have them. Examples are *all*, *none*, *some*, *either*, *neither* and *any*, which we have discussed with demonstrative pronouns but which might also be called indefinite.

Apart from these, the indefinite pronouns include the words *enough*, *each* and *other*, which are also adjectives, and *aught*, *naught* and *else*, which cannot be used as adjectives. Indefinite pronouns might also include *every*, and certainly must include *it*. Each of these two words, though, demands a little section to itself.

"EVERY"

Every is here called a pronoun, as it used to be a pronoun rather than an adjective. Originally it was an abbreviation of "ever-each." Shakespeare used it as a simple pronoun and not as an adjective—"Every of your wishes"—and yet today its use is entirely adjectival.

The most important thing to remember about *every* is that it is a singular word. It is most curious that while everyone naturally and correctly says "Put everything in its place" he probably says also "Everyone has to be in their seats by seven o'clock."

The senseless feature of this construction is that, although the singularity of *everyone* is acknowledged by the use of *has*, the general muddle-headedness is shown by the misuse of the personal possessive pronoun *their*.

Lewis Carroll made the Duchess say: "If everybody minded their own business, the world would go round a deal faster than it does." The author of *Alice*, however, was quoting, and is not to be accused of ignorance in himself.

The difficulty with the words *everyone*, *everybody* and *nobody* is in using an accompanying pronoun to cover both sexes. The correct construction would be: "Everyone has to be in his or her seat . . . " or "If everybody minded his or her own business . . ."

If that sounds clumsy to you, why not use *his* alone? In baby books and in various aspects of law and medicine the masculine personal pronouns are understood to apply to both genders. If, then, you dislike the "his or her" construction, I advise you to say: "Everybody should mind his own business." There are sound precedents for this practice in other languages.

"IT"

A very hardworked little word is *it*. In its normal use it is an impersonal pronoun (as opposed to a personal pronoun): "The door was open when I passed the first time, but when I passed the second time *it* was shut."

Apart from this, however, *it* has many other applications. Often the governing noun is understood, as in "Give it up," when *it* is the problem or the battle.

Nobody can explain the significance of *it* in "It frequently happens . . ." But in "It is a rainy day" *it* means "the day," for it would sound odd to say "The day is a rainy day." We cannot say what *it* is, however, in "It is raining."

It defies us there. It almost defies us in such sentences as "Let's rough it" and "It's up to you," but here we know that *it* takes the place of some vague subject or object which is unknown. (Subject and object are discussed in the next chapter.)

It also enables us to avoid unrelated participles, of which I shall have much more to say later. For example, study the sentence: "It being assumed that the bridge is finished in time, the first train will cross the river in August." If we were slipshod grammarians we should say, absurdly: "Assuming that the bridge is finished in time, the first train . . ."

To conclude this chapter, I shall repeat one important piece of instruction about *it*. *It's* is short for "It is," as in "It's sunny." The possessive of *it* is *its*, as in "its colour," "its size."

CHAPTER VI

The Sentence and the Paragraph

* *

I_F grammar is the basis of language, the sentence is the basis of grammar. A passage of true prose is composed of a series of sentences, each sentence being connected in some way or other with the preceding sentence. The whole series of sentences should show the writer's train of thought in that particular passage. When the writer wants to switch to another train of thought he may, for convenience, and for lucidity, start a fresh paragraph, but I shall deal with this matter later in the chapter.

DEFINITION OF A SENTENCE

A sentence, according to my personal definition, is a complete statement. By this I mean that, to make sense, it must consist of, at least, a subject and a verb. A string of words between two full-stops is thus not necessarily a sentence, even though a section of the popular Press would have it so.

I insist, therefore, that a sentence is a *complete* statement. "I live," though a simple statement, is a complete statement and a perfectly good sentence. Too often we read incoherent passages like this:

"Jane wanted a dog. A real dog. No matter what kind of dog. Just a dog. A dog that would be her own pal."

In that collection of words there is only one sentence—"Jane wanted a dog."

I despair when I read business letters that start like this: "Referring to your letter of the 16th November." After the full-stop the reader is left groping in mid-air, for these words obviously do not make a sentence. After "November" there should be a comma, followed by a proper noun or a pronoun attached to the present participle "referring."

Thus, such a sentence might be the following: "Referring to your letter of the 16th November, I am surprised to learn that the account is still unpaid."

But even when there is an attempt to complete the sentence, the comma is followed by a noun or pronoun which is not attached, and could not possibly be attached, to the participle. We all read "sentences" like this almost every day of our lives: "Referring to your letter of the 16th November, the horse was sold last Monday." Literally, this means that while the horse was being sold the animal was referring to the letter.

The common misuse of participles, however, is a subject to which I shall devote more attention in a later chapter.

SLOVENLY EXAMPLES

While on the subject of so-called sentences which are not sentences, I should like to give some actual examples from respectable newspapers which rather pride themselves on their English.

"Mr. and Mrs. —— —— were the stars at Guildhall Art Gallery yesterday afternoon. Invisible stars except for the early arrivals."

"I wrote on Monday that the Planning Committee had agreed in principle to a plaque costing between £5,000 and £10,000. This in addition to a memorial already in Princesshay."

"Canada seems the right place to hold such a celebration— the Hereford is still comfortably the most popular beef breed of the New World. This though that Scots interloper, the Aberdeen Angus, is steadily improving its position."

One of my cuttings is from a Sunday paper, in which a reviewer describes a Japanese novel "translated into easy but not very elegant English by an American." The reviewer's own English is not very elegant, either, for later in the same review she writes:

"But some people like . . . to think of the Inquisition as a medieval bogy good for a shiver and not the beastly mechanism that creaked its way into the nineteenth century. To whom the book may be recommended."

It is easy to find grammatical faults in trade circulars, and it may be unfair to give the following example immediately after an example from a writer who should know better. I mean no disrespect to the reputable firm concerned, and this extract from its joinery catalogue is a typical example of the kind of writing that should be avoided in trade publications:

"Delivery can be given immediately from stock of all . . . . illustrated in this catalogue. All External Joinery being supplied primed all round with genuine red lead paint."

As it stands, the second part of the passage is not a sentence, but replacement of "being" by "is" would make it correct. Incidentally, the unnecessary use of capitals in "External Joinery" is a typical example of the indiscriminate use of capitals in trade publications of all kinds, except, perhaps, trade journals, which often show a good standard of grammar.

SUBJECT AND PREDICATE

Most of us probably remember how at school we were taught to divide a sentence into "subject and predicate," and this division is quite useful as long as it is understood.

The *subject* of a sentence is the person or thing the statement is about. In our simple sentence, "I live," the pronoun "I" is the subject. Generally, the subject comes before the verb, but sometimes, for the sake of a special effect, the order is reversed. "Came the dawn" is a familiar example of this *inversion*, as it is called, and in this case "the dawn" is the subject.

The *predicate* is the part of the sentence following the subject, and *must* contain the verb. Although the word itself has several meanings, which you can find out from any English dictionary, its derivation, from the Latin *praedicare* (to proclaim) immediately gives its meaning as applied to grammar. It is the predicate which *proclaims* what the sentence is about.

In the sentence, "I live," it is the predicate "live" which gives meaning to the statement and completes the sentence. But this is a very short, if effective, sentence, and every day we use or read sentences which are not only longer but also more complex.

LONGER SENTENCES

For the moment, however, let us avoid complexity and consider such longer simple sentences as the following.

(a) "I live in a house."
(b) "He gave a pound."
(c) "The tree grows near the stream."
(d) "She loves books."

Division of these sentences into subject and predicate gives:

Subject   *Predicate*
(a) "I   live [*verb*] in a house."
(b) "He   gave [*verb*] a pound."
(c) "The tree grows [*verb*] near the stream."
(d) "She   loves [*verb*] books."

Further examination of these sentences shows the presence of two kinds of predicate, the difference being determined by the kind of verb. Verbs of the (b) and (d) kind are *transitive* while verbs of the (a) and (c) kind are *intransitive*. We discussed these terms in Chapter IV, and therefore need say little more about them here. It is worth remembering, nevertheless, that even though a complex sentence may consist of several sub-sentences, each of the sub-sentences can be divided into subject and predicate.

THE OBJECT OF A SENTENCE

Several times in this book I have referred to the *object* of a sentence, and it may be clear by now what is meant by the term. The object is the part of a sentence affected by the subject through a transitive verb.

In the simple sentence, "I eat bread," *bread* is the object. In examples (a) and (d) above the objects are *a pound* and *books*.

It is not essential for every sentence to have an object. "I eat" is a perfectly good sentence on its own, without an object.

An intransitive verb, of course, cannot be followed by an object. Examples of intransitive verbs are *sleep, lie, stand, sit, walk, swim, come, go, run, live* and *fly*. (There is a transitive form of *run* in the sense of running an organisation.) A construction like "Walk a mile" or "Swim the river" does not make its verb transitive, for the subject is not really doing anything *to* the mile or the river.

Some verbs can be either transitive or intransitive. In our example (*c*), above, where there is no object, *grows* is intransitive. In "The gardener grows cucumbers," the verb is transitive, with *cucumbers* as the object.

The object of a sentence need not follow the transitive verb. In the sentence, "Pale hands I loved," the object is *hands*, for this is another kind of inversion.

SUBJECTIVE AND OBJECTIVE PRONOUNS

In Chapter IV we discussed the subjective and objective forms of the personal pronouns. In the use of pronouns, the subjective form is often wrongly used for the object, and you hear misconstructions like:

"He took Mother and I for a ride in the car."

"The manager met my friend and I at the station."

In both sentences *I* should be *me*. People who are not sure of their English sometimes try to get over the difficulty by using *myself*: "Those present at the meeting included the mayor, Mr. A, Mr. B, Mrs. C, Miss D, and myself."

I should point out here that a preposition is always followed by the objective form of a personal pronoun, so that "Between you and me" is correct. The following should make you shudder, and rightly so:

"Between you and I . . ."

"Come and sit beside we girls."

In the B.B.C. Children's Hour (of all things!) I was horrified to hear: "My husband shouted to Michael and I one evening . . ." This must have slipped past several people connected with the programme.

Misuse of the subjective forms of the personal pronouns is one of the commonest mistakes in English. Less common is the misuse of the objective forms, although the dreadful use of *them* ("Them's the best") is widespread. Regional peculiarities of dialect also produce errors, but these are forgivable.

In concluding this section I must remind you of the peculiarities of the verb *to be* described in Chapter IV on page 52. Thus, "It is I" is strangely correct.

CLAUSES AND PHRASES

A *clause* (as explained in Chapter III, page 26) is a short complete sentence forming part of a longer sentence. It must, therefore, contain a subject and a verb.

A *phrase* is a group of words *not* containing a verb, and which may or may not form part of a clause or sentence. Far too often the term *phrase* is ignorantly used for a clause.

COMPOUND SENTENCES

By a compound sentence I mean a sentence composed of two or more clauses suitably connected. Here is an example:

"John went for a walk and met Bob, who was shopping for his mother."

This is composed of the following sentences, each of which is complete in itself: "John went for a walk. John met Bob. Bob was shopping for his mother."

LENGTHS OF SENTENCES

The sentences forming a passage of prose should be neither too short nor too long, unless the writer is aiming at some special effect. In a book of instruction, such as this book, for example, short sentences may be advisable. Sentences which are too short sound jerky and are irritating to the reader or listener. Sentences which are too long soon cause the reader or listener to clamour for a rest, and the main matter of the sentence may be forgotten.

The ideal length for a sentence is that which makes the reader or listener aware of smoothness of flow, and gives him time to collect his thoughts at suitable intervals. The consistently short sentences in some of the popular newspapers are similar in form to the short sentences found in very young children's reading-books, and writing for adults in this manner is not to be encouraged. At the other extreme are long, involved sentences which could do with much pruning and revision—sentences containing elaborate parentheses and collections of clauses and phrases—and these are not to be encouraged, either.

I am not implying that all the sentences in a prose passage should be of equal length. That would be dull, even if it could be achieved. The writer's aim should be to convey his meaning not merely by a string of facts and opinions, but as smoothly and rhythmically—as musically, if you like—as he can within his capabilities.

I cannot teach you how to become a writer—nobody can do that, for real writers are born—but I hope I can help you to write and speak decent grammatical English, and in the judging of suitable lengths for sentences there is nothing like constant practice.

When you have written a passage of prose, read it over as though you were hearing it read. Consider each sentence not in itself but as part of the passage. Then adjust it, putting in a conjunction here and a parenthesis there, removing an *and* and inserting a full-stop, replacing a comma by a semi-colon. Do not be too lazy to write it all over again—remember that striving for perfection is one of the things that distinguish the artist from the craftsman.

It is a good idea, if time allows, to revise your writing after a month's rest. You may then be able to notice defects you never saw before.

Before concluding this section I should like to give a warning. A friend of mine was attending a series of classes in free-lance journalism, conducted by a writer whose experience and ability, I gathered, were limited to writing of a somewhat low standard. His maxim was: "Keep your sentences short," and by "short" he meant really short, short to the point of scrappiness, and compound sentences were discouraged. The efforts of this man appeared in the less enlightened provincial weekly Press, and my warning is against such false and wholly misleading teaching.

CONNECTING THE PARTS OF A SENTENCE

In Chapter III there was quite a long explanation of the parts of speech called *conjunctions*. I said that conjunctions, besides linking parts of a sentence, also express something in themselves. Thus, the separate clauses in a sentence can be connected by conjunctions, the choice of conjunctions depending on the writer's or the speaker's meaning.

For exercise, let us try to rewrite the following group of jerky sentences.

"I left the house. I thought it was half-past eight. It was a wet morning. It was warm. Few people were about. I could not understand this. I caught a bus. The bus was half-empty. The bus took me to the station. My train was usually at the platform. This morning it wasn't. I looked at the station clock. I realised my mistake. I had got up an hour too early."

That passage sounds most depressing as it stands, but its style is not uncommon. We could rewrite it like this:

"I thought it was half-past eight when I left the house one wet but warm morning, and could not understand why so few people were about. I caught a half-empty bus which took me to the station, and although my train was usually at the platform, this morning it wasn't. On looking at the station clock I realised my mistake. I had got up an hour too early."

I think you will agree that the second version is easier and more pleasant to read than the series of unconnected statements of the first version. There are fourteen sentences in the passage, which we have rewritten in four sentences.

We have used a few conjunctions—*and, although, but*. We have used some relative pronouns—*when* and *which*. The fifth and sixth sentences have been replaced by the clause ". . . and could not understand why so few people were about." The use of the present participle "On looking . . ." telescopes two sentences into one.

PARENTHESIS

A parenthesis is a word, clause, sentence or phrase inserted in a sentence that is grammatically complete without it. A simple example is in the sentence: "The party's prospects—alas!—have been ruined by the irresponsible actions of a few hotheads."

The word "alas!" is the parenthesis. In this example it is separated from the rest of the sentence by two dashes, which themselves are called parentheses. Parenthesis can also be indicated by brackets or by commas. Besides round brackets there are square brackets which also have their use, but I shall deal with this in more detail in Chapter VIII.

A whole sentence, or even a whole paragraph, can sometimes with advantage be placed in parentheses in the midst of a passage of prose.

Besides its use for the interpolation of something, however, parenthesis can be a means of linking parts of a sentence, and when skilfully applied it can be effective, thus:

"The state of the country at that time—there had been six major industrial strikes in two years—was parlous. Repeated demands for higher wages, demands which without exception were meekly accepted, had resulted in undisguised inflation. Tax-dodging was on the increase, and the corrupt prospered while the honest struggled along in vain. The economy of the country was at a low ebb, and exports for the year in question (worth £10,000,000 five years before) had dwindled by over 50 per cent."

In that passage there are three examples of parenthesis—that between the dashes ("there had . . . two years"), that between commas ("demands which . . . meekly accepted"), and that between brackets ("worth . . . before").

I should like to stress that a parenthesis should not be so long as to be unwieldy. In the Press and in books you will sometimes see atrocious examples, consisting of whole auxiliary passages complete with full stops, semi-colons and commas, placed in brackets or between dashes. The need for such painful constructions is obviated by the use of a little care and some rewriting, and although busy daily journals have an excuse in lack of time, contributors to monthly magazines and writers of books cannot make the same plea.

SYNTAX

There may be several grammatical ways in English of arranging the clauses, phrases, and words in a sentence to result in the same meaning. The subject of arrangement is known as *syntax*, and ideally the arrangement to choose is that which reads the most smoothly and rhythmically while clearly expressing the sense. In this respect English is fairly flexible.

Although it is not true that almost any sentence can be rearranged, it is easy to pick out sentences that have a number of possibilities. Consider the following.

"The children's party will as usual be held in the church hall on Boxing Day."

"In the church hall on Boxing Day will be held the usual party for children."

"On Boxing Day, in the church hall, the usual party for children will be held."

"The usual Boxing Day children's party will be held in the church hall."

Other arrangements may suggest themselves to you. These sentences are all variations of the same theme, and all give the correct meaning. Personally, I think the last sentence sounds the most pleasant.

If alternative forms of order give confusing or ambiguous results, those are the forms to avoid. For instance, could we have said "the usual children's party"? We could, but only at the cost of ambiguity. This construction could imply that the same children were always invited to the party, and so we avoid the ambiguity by saying "the usual party for children" or "the usual Boxing Day children's party."

"ONLY"

A word frequently used in the wrong place is *only*. Every day you hear such sentences as :"I only arrived here three hours ago." The speaker means that up to the present his stay has been short, and the word *only* refers to *three hours*, so that the sentence should be: "I arrived here only three hours ago."

Only arrived, strictly, is a belittlement of the act of arriving, as if arriving was of no importance. In this particular sentence, fortunately, this is clearly not the speaker's meaning, and hence no ambiguity results from the misplacing of *only*. But in other sentences there could easily be ambiguity, as, for example, in the following. The correct constructions are in brackets.

"I only offered five pounds for it and she looked insulted." ("I offered only five pounds . . . .")

"Coloured people only live on the island." ("Only coloured people . . . .")

"Children will only be admitted if accompanied by adults." ("Children will be admitted only if . . . .")

"There will only be a strike in the factory if the sacked men are not reinstated." ("There will be a strike in the factory only if . . . .")

"I only knocked him down when he became aggressive." ("I knocked him down only when . . . .")

"ALSO"

A word which can easily be used ambiguously is *also*. Consider the sentence, "They also serve who only stand and wait," from Milton's "On his Blindness."

Only is used correctly, but *also* may be associated with *they* or with *serve*. If it is associated with *they*, there is an implication that other people are serving more actively, but that they who only stand and wait are serving, too.

If *also* is associated with the verb *serve*, the sentence means that while they are standing and waiting they are *also* serving.

In speech, a hint as to the meaning could be given by accentuation, so that if the first meaning was intended stress could be laid on *they*, and if the second meaning was intended stress could be laid on *serve*. We are sure that Milton had the first meaning in mind.

Another example of the ambiguity of *also* is in this passage: "We went to Devon and met my aunt and uncle, who had been to Cornwall. During our holiday we also went to Cornwall, and then to Dorset." *Also* can be associated with *we* or with *Cornwall*.

Now consider the use of *also* in such a sentence as the following: "I gave her an apple, a pear, an orange, and also a peach." You might think that *also* after *and* is unnecessary. So it is, if the speaker is simply enumerating the fruits he gave. But if the speaker's intention is to emphasise his generosity, and to imply that the recipient has done very well to get the first three fruits, then *also* after *and* may be justified.

At other times *also* is even used in place of *and*, as in: "We bought all kinds of Christmas presents—toys, books, games, also things to wear." *Also* here is not only wrong but clumsy.

PARAGRAPHS

A passage of prose is divided into *paragraphs*, as we all know, the first sentence of a new paragraph being started on a fresh line and "inset" slightly to warn the reader that a new paragraph is about to begin.

Generally, the start of a new paragraph should indicate a deviation, or a break, in the sequence of thoughts and ideas. I

emphasise the adverb *generally*, because the "rule" I have given
—if it can be called a rule—*is* general. The arrangement of
sentences in paragraphs is also convenient, gives a more pleasing
appearance than a solid block of prose, and tends to make reading easy.

How long should paragraphs be? To this enquiry, no ready
answer can be given, for much depends on the kind of prose in
question. In the daily Press, paragraphs are fairly short. In fact,
they are often too short, but the Press has a valid excuse. A
newspaper is made up in a hurry; sections often have to be discarded or changed in position, and a short paragraph of type is
easier to manipulate or move elsewhere than would be a more
solid block.

There is less excuse in the weekly papers, and in the more
popular weeklies short paragraphs are too prevalent. In numerous cases you will see paragraphs consisting of only one or two
short sentences, but I suspect that this practice, like the cult of
the strip pictures ("comic strips"), is to suit the semi-literate and
lazy-minded readers.

In works of instruction or edification it is helpful to keep
the paragraphs as short as possible without spoiling the flow of
ideas or the appearance of the page, and in this book my aim is
to do this.

It is conventional to start a new paragraph at the start of
quoted speech, especially in fictional writing, even if the speech
consists only of an exclamation like "Ah!"

In non-fictional works paragraphs should not be made too
long even if the flow of ideas is continuous. A whole page of
unbroken type can look forbidding, and if there is no natural
break or deviation it is better to make an artificial one. Two or
three paragraphs on a page of manuscript, typescript or print
look better than a page of scrappy paragraphs and better than
no paragraphs at all.

What of letters? A typed business letter should consist of
relatively short paragraphs, as the recipient will probably have
dozens of such letters to read in a day and the sender should try
to make his task easy.

I am not going to advise you on the writing of your private
letters, for that would be impertinent. The arrangement and tone
of a personal letter, however, depend on whom it is written to;
thus, you could say the same things to *B* in a very different way

from the manner and arrangement in which you could say them to *A*, even to the extent of making your paragraphs longer or shorter.

ARRANGEMENT OF IDEAS

An idea is something that occurs to one—a thought, a mental image, a notion, a conception, a supposition, a plan, a view, an intention, or just an opinion. An idea that comes into one's head may be the result of a preceding idea, and may give rise to one following.

In writing, or in speech of some length, ideas should be expressed in some order. That is, do not try to write or say anything just as it comes to your mind. Marshall your ideas, put them in order, and be selective.

In a long impromptu speech it is not as easy to do this as in writing, or in a prepared speech, and some speakers, experienced in the art, are better at arrangement of ideas than others. Statesmen's replies in Parliament, and judicial speeches in court, are often wonderful examples of unprepared speech at its best.

I assume that you are neither a statesman nor a legal light, and that your speech is confined to ordinary conversation at its various levels. No doubt, however, you often have to write, and in writing you have the chance of planning and revision denied to ready speakers. Then use the chance, and make the most of it. Do as I have advised above: marshall your ideas, put them in the logical order (or the most logical), and be selective.

By being selective, I mean that you should not be afraid of throwing out a sentence, a clause, or a phrase, as long as the sense remains and the passage can do without it. Try to lead the reader from one idea to the next. If there is to be a contrast, or a change of mood, build up to it with all the resources— facts, deductions and theories—at your command. If a conclusion is to be drawn, try to influence the reader to see it as you see it.

The foregoing, I am afraid, is all very general advice. To give examples would be an unending, almost impossible, task, and to gain appreciation of the niceties of exposition there is nothing like constant reading and practice.

ECONOMY

In the previous section I said that you should not be afraid of throwing out anything as long as the sense remains and the passage can do without it. Economy, in fact, is an essential virtue in good writing, and, like the arrangement of ideas, can only be achieved with practice.

For many years I have had the job of writing 1,800 words a month on nine or ten topics for a monthly magazine. It is great fun, for that job, more than anything, has taught me how to economise in words. In some kinds of writing you can spread yourself—in a novel, for instance, or in a letter to an intimate friend.

In a short story or an essay, on the other hand, you are more restricted, but restricted only in one field. When you are restricted in nine or ten fields it is not so easy, for it means that on each topic all inessential writing has to be ruthlessly cut out.

RULES FOR ECONOMY

If asked to give rules for economy I should arrange them under the following headings.

Circumlocution. Avoid "circumlocutions"—that is, things said in a roundabout way. For example, "most of" is preferable to "the major part of," and "the poor" is preferable to "the lower-income groups." I have seen a notice, "Please deposit unwanted articles in the receptacle provided," on which some language-conscious person has written: "Please throw rubbish into the bin." Interpolated clauses and phrases, like "It cannot be denied that" and "in the act of" can take up valuable space.

Use of adjectives. Avoid unnecessary adjectives, as in "arid desert," "inspissated gloom," "silvery moon," "slippery ice." You might just as reasonably talk of "wet water."

Nevertheless, you should make full use of helpful or explanatory adjectives. There are numerous adjectives which, skilfully used, can save half a dozen or more words of description.

There is nothing to prevent you, also, from using compound adjectives, unless they are clumsy. For the sake of economy I should permit "face-saving action," "ninety-year-old Mrs. Smith," "the newly-married couple," "the public-spirited city

council." Above, I have used "language-conscious person."
Shakespeare had his "lily-liver'd loon."

By "clumsy" I mean such laboured constructions as "opera-
tion-famous surgeon," "sea-encircled island," "risen-from-the-
foam Venus," "greatly-to-be-admired heroine," "universally-
acclaimed book." The use of such heavy adjectives is not to be
encouraged.

You will notice that compound adjectives are made up of two
or more *hyphenated* words. I shall deal with this practice more
fully in Chapter VIII.

Use of parenthesis. Make use of smooth parenthetical phrases,
clauses and minor sentences in such a way that ideas, statements
and explanations can be slipped into major sentences. I insist
on smoothness; the parenthesis should be so unobtrusive as to
be hardly noticeable.

Digressions. If your writing is confined to a definite amount of
space, keep digressions to a minimum. Digressions—and I do
not mean "padding"—may be perfectly justified if you have
room for them and they are relevant to your subject. Too often,
I am afraid, a writer inserts a digression out of vanity or egoism.
Sometimes a digression comes perilously close to padding.

Padding. Avoid padding absolutely. Of all the sins of speech
and writing it is one of the most recognisable, even though it
may be quite grammatical. I need not detail the many forms
padding can take, for you have only to pick up a newspaper and
read some dreary speech to find it.

Padding is the vice of using strings of words, sentences and
paragraphs and saying absolutely nothing, or at any rate nothing
of value. It is a very easy vice to acquire, but writers and
speakers can only "fool some of the people some of the time."

NUMERALS

If a sentence starts with a number the number must be
written in words, thus:

"Fifty years ago there were fewer cars on the roads."

"Twenty-three bags of corn were stolen from the barn last
night."

"Nineteen thirty-nine was the year of fate."

If a number is *quoted* in speech it should also be written in
words, as in the following examples:

" 'Sir,' I said, 'I have to report the arrival of a hundred and twenty-two cases of stores.' "

"When I asked his date of birth he replied, 'The twenty-ninth of February, nineteen forty-eight.' "

CONCLUSION

I started this chapter by talking about the sentence, and find I have wandered somewhat to the extent of talking about prose in general. All prose—and all verse, for that matter—springs from the sentence, however, and I hope that my deviations from the main subject have not been in vain. I could have said much more, but shall deal with further interesting points, and shall amplify matters already touched, in later chapters.

CHAPTER VII

Punctuation

◆◆◆◆◆◆◆◆◆◆◆◆◆◆◆◆◆◆◆◆◆◆◆◆◆◆◆◆◆◆◆◆◆◆◆◆◆◆

Punctuation literally means *pointing* (Latin, *punctus*, a point), and in grammar it is the name given to the division of statements, or collections of words, into sentences, clauses, phrases, questions, quotations and exclamations.

Speech is punctuated by pauses of different length, by the speaker's tone of voice, by inflection, by emphasis, by facial expression, and, in the case of questions, by the order of words. In writing, however, there is the advantage of a series of *punctuation marks*, marks which are more than mere conventions as, used intelligently, they can give meaning to prose or verse and prevent misunderstanding.

Without punctuation, a sentence or paragraph would be like a telegram—and the inadequacy of telegram language is demonstrated by the necessity for the inclusion of costly instructions like STOP, COMMA and QUERY.

Punctuation can be regarded as guidance to the reader. In punctuation, therefore, I include the use of capital letters and, in printing, the use of *italics*.

THE PUNCTUATION MARKS

The punctuation marks in English consist of the following:

Full-stop .	Single quotation marks ' '
Comma ,	Double quotation marks " "
Semi-colon ;	Hyphen -
Colon :	Dash —
Question mark ?	Round brackets ( )
Exclamation mark !	Square brackets [ ]

There is also the apostrophe ('), and I might include marks of omission (. . . .).

THE FULL-STOP

Everybody knows that the full-stop is used at the end of a sentence. It should indicate, in fact, that the sentence has come to a *stop*. Yet too often we come across letters that start like this: "Referring to your letter of the 12th February." This collection of words is not a sentence, and after the full-stop the reader is left floundering.

After "February" there should be a comma, followed by the noun or pronoun attached to the present participle "Referring". A correct construction would thus consist of something like this: "Referring to your letter of the 12th February, we regret to say that the work has not yet been done." An *incorrect* construction would be: "Referring to your letter of the 12th February, the work has not yet been done." This means, quite absurdly, that the work has been referring to your letter.

There is a type of prose, not only in the popular Press but also in the works of accepted modern novelists, in which the structure of proper sentences seems to be scorned. This slovenliness produces the kind of English displayed on page 71, a kind which I certainly do not wish to encourage.

THE FULL-STOP WITH ABBREVIATIONS

As is commonly known, the full-stop is sometimes used to denote abbreviations. Some pedants allow the full-stop only to those abbreviations which are parts of words, and *not* to those abbreviations in which the first and last letters of words are given. Thus, exponents of this practice would allow *Mr, Mrs* and *Dr,* but would insist on the full-stop with *Jan., Sept., Mon.* and *Yorks.*

I prefer, however, to give the full-stop to nearly all abbreviations whether or not the first and last letters are given, and typical abbreviations are the following:

Titles	Mr., Mrs., Prof., Gen.
Months and days	Feb., Dec., Tues., Thurs.
Units of measurement	In. (*not* ins.), ft., cwt. (*not* cwts.,) cm. (*not* cms.), oz (*not* ozs.), lb. (*not* lbs.).

There are also the innumerable cases in which full-stops are used with initial letters to indicate abbreviations. In some quarters, unfortunately, there is a growing practice to omit the full-stop, and in some of the publications of the British Broadcasting Corporation the Corporation calls itself the BBC instead of the B.B.C.

Some publishers and printers insist on placing full-stops after Roman numerals, as in "Henry VI.," "Charles I." and "Elizabeth II." The only justification for this that I can see is the avoidance of confusion between the Roman numeral I. and the pronoun *I*.

It should be remembered that *per cent.* is an abbreviation of *per centum*, and needs the full-stop.

Incidentally, if an abbreviation comes at the end of a sentence there should logically be two full-stops—the first for the abbreviation and the second to mark the end of the sentence. In practice, nevertheless, it is conventional to make one full-stop do for the two.

THE COMMA

The comma is a very useful little mark. Less abrupt than the full-stop, it can mark the end of a clause or a phrase within a sentence and give a hint that there is something to follow.

While the correct use of the comma is fairly well understood, there is a tendency either to use too many commas or not enough. Here are two examples, one of each failing:

Too many commas

"It was a fine day, and the sun was hot. As I walked through the meadow, towards the river, I heard the cuckoo, whose call followed me wherever I walked, but who seemed intent on eluding me. For an instant I spied him, perched on top of a tall elm, but when he knew that he was spotted, he flew off again. I reached the water's edge, and took off my shoes and socks."

There is no misuse of commas in this passage, but there is an effect of jerkiness. The passage would be smoother, easier to read, if it was rewritten in this way:

"It was a fine day, and the sun was hot. As I walked through the meadow towards the river I heard the cuckoo, whose call followed me wherever I walked but who seemed intent on eluding me. For an instant I spied him perched on top of a tall elm, but when he knew that he was spotted he flew off again.

I reached the water's edge and took off my shoes and socks."

Not enough commas

"The Member for Moontown in the Commons today in an amendment proposed that the duty on imported sealing-wax be raised by six per cent. as from January 1 to conform with the inflated cost of production in Commonwealth countries.

"The Member for Sunville supporting the amendment said that as a director of a sealing-wax company in this country he thought that every effort should be made to stop overseas competition. The President of the Board of Trade in his reply said there was no evidence of any adverse effect on the sealing-wax market of competitive imports, and although he had not been informed of any complaints from the trade he was appointing a special sub-committee to investigate the whole question."

In its mad rush along this passage is just as irritating as the previous passage which suffered from an excess of commas. The reader is left breathless. The following calmer version shows that only a few commas are necessary:

"The Member for Moontown, in the Commons today, in an amendment, proposed that the duty on imported sealing-wax be raised by six per cent. as from January 1, to conform with the inflated cost of production in Commonwealth countries.

"The Member for Sunville, supporting the amendment, said that as a director of a sealing-wax company in this country he thought that every effort should be made to stop overseas competition. The President of the Board of Trade, in his reply, said there was no evidence of any adverse effect on the sealing-wax market of competitive imports, and, although he had not been informed of any complaints from the trade, he was appointing a special sub-committee to investigate the whole question."

Legal documents, of course, are notorious for their lack of commas. This failing is said to have originated in the days of old when scriveners were paid on piecework and the insertion of commas wasted valuable time. There is no doubt that legal documents would be more comprehensible if they were properly punctuated.

COMMAS IN ENUMERATION

It is modern accepted practice to omit the last comma before *and* in an enumeration, thus:

"They brought gifts of flowers, fruit, clothing, toys and money to the refugees."

Indeed, whether or not you accept the custom, and whether or not you prefer to write ". . . toys, and money . . . ," some publishers and editors insist in their style-sheets on the omission of the final comma. An exception would be made in the case of possible ambiguity or doubt, as in:

"The train will stop at Harrow, Pinner, Northwood, Watford, and Bushey."

"Watford and Bushey" might be interpreted as the name of a single station, just as "Harrow and Wealdstone" is one station.

Another case where the last comma would be justified, even essential, is in: "The motion received the support of the Bishops of Durham, Winchester, Grantham, Bath and Wells, and Newcastle."

ENUMERATIONS FORMING SUBJECTS OF SENTENCES

Where the enumerated items collectively form the subject of a sentence preceding a verb, the insertion of a comma *after* the last item depends largely upon personal preference.

We can write: "All books, magazines, papers and other publications must be submitted to the censor for examination."

I think this is preferable to, and reads more smoothly than, the following: "All books, magazines, papers and other publications, must be submitted to the censor for examination."

In the second example it can be argued that the comma after "publications" is necessary for grouping the items of the subject, but to my mind the grouping is given by the first two commas and the word "and."

Now consider the following passage:

"Strong sense of duty, sympathetic regard for the feelings of others, high moral purpose and understanding of different points of view were the qualities for which the leader was loved."

In this passage each item is a group of words. It would probably be spoken with a natural pause after each item. The result would be better, then, with a comma after "purpose" and another comma after "view."

CONFUSING ENUMERATIONS

Confusing examples of enumerations occur in the daily Press, especially where names of dignitaries are accompanied by explanatory phrases. Frequently this kind of reporting appears:

"A civic reception was held at the Town Hall to-day, when the Lord Mayor, Ald. Henry Skrimpton, the Lady Mayoress, Ald. James Todd, the Sheriff, and Mrs. Todd, entertained the members of the Bongoland Expedition to lunch. The guests included Col. G. Dykes, leader of the expedition, his chief assistant, Major P. Hamm, Dr. A. Grayling, the chief scientist and technical adviser, Mr. W. Jones, meteorological officer, the expedition's botanist, Mr. S. Crumm, the supplies officer; Mr. H. Lawrence, Mr. K. Smollett, treasurer and secretary, and Dr. Leonard Foxhall, medical officer."

At a casual reading the list is not easy to understand. Information of this nature is better tabulated, but apart from considerations of space (tabulation in a newspaper takes up precious room), the reporter probably thinks it more literary to make a continuous prose passage of the information.

The news item would be more intelligible if use was made of (*a*) brackets or of (*b*) semi-colons, thus:

(*a*) "The guests included Col. G. Dykes (leader of the expedition), Major P. Hamm (his chief assistant), Dr. A. Grayling (the chief scientist and technical adviser), ..." and so on.

(*b*) "The guests included: Col. G. Dykes, leader of the expedition; Major P. Hamm, his chief assistant; Dr. A. Grayling, the chief scientist and technical adviser; . . . ." and so on.

PARENTHETICAL USE OF COMMAS

In the original version of the above list of civic guests, some of the commas are used parenthetically. That is (as you will recall from the last chapter), the words in parenthesis could have been omitted without any destruction of the sense, the parenthetical phrases being "leader of the expedition," "Major P. Hamm," "the chief scientist and technical adviser," and so on to "medical officer."

In this particular case, of course, as I showed in the revised versions, it would have been more reasonable to stick to a definite order, with each name followed by its bearer's function in the expedition. One revision allows the semi-colons, these being stronger than the commas, to control the groupings. The other revision, with brackets, allows the writer to retain a parenthetical construction.

The parenthetical use of commas is common. In my preceding paragraph the phrase "of course" was between parenthetical commas. Other examples (with the parenthetical words in *italics*) are the following:

"The inherent vagaries of mining are too well known, but, *subject to this qualification,* the unofficial prediction of success may be accepted."

"In Congolia, a prolific weed, *the water-hyacinth,* has made its appearance." (Note the correct use of the hyphen. A "water hyacinth" would be a hyacinth made of water.)

"Peter Paul Rubens (1577–1640), *the greatest painter of the Flemish School,* was born at Siegen in Nassau."

It is unnecessary to give any more such examples, but I might add that clauses starting with relative pronouns, when inserted in sentences, are also parenthetical, as in the following:

"His frightening experience, which nearly cost him his life, left him a nervous wreck."

"Stratford-on-Avon, where Shakespeare was born in 1564, is a picturesque little town."

"The year 1314, when the independence of Scotland was established at Bannockburn, was a milestone in British history."

The parenthetical use of commas, then, should be easily understood. But in using commas in this way the writer must not forget that he is using a parenthesis, and a very common mistake is to omit the second comma. Let us rewrite wrongly two of our examples:

"The inherent vagaries of mining are too well known, but, subject to this qualification the unofficial prediction of success may be accepted."

"In Congolia a prolific weed, the water-hyacinth has made its appearance."

The trouble is that the comma has so many uses, and is so inconspicuous, that it is apt to be overlooked. Now, if we chose to use brackets instead of commas for our passages in parenthesis, we should never dream of omitting the second bracket; so why omit the second comma?

The possibility of confusion when essential commas are omitted can be illustrated by the following examples:

"In 1926 I was told there had been an epidemic."

"In 1926, I was told, there had been an epidemic." The first sentence is ambiguous. Was it 1926 when the writer was told of the epidemic? The correctly-punctuated second sentence makes the meaning perfectly clear.

Sometimes, though more rarely, you even come across an omission of the first comma. Here is an extract from a published definition of an inn:

". . . an establishment held out by the proprietor as offering food, drink, and if required, sleeping accommodation, ..."

The words "if required" are a parenthesis, and there should be a comma after "and."

If one comma of the parenthesis is omitted, so should the other be omitted, and many parenthetic words and phrases can safely be used without commas. An example is "therefore," as in: "I therefore should be grateful for the return of the map." Unfortunately many Civil Service typists seem to have been taught a silly rule about "therefore," a rule resulting in such stilted sentences as: "I, therefore, should be glad if you would advise me by return of the amount of interest from this investment."

TWO SMALL MATTERS

To conclude this section on the parenthetical use of commas, two small matters should be mentioned.

First, in the writing of dates in a prose passage, the year should be given parenthetically between commas, as in: "On the 21st June, 1946, and again on the 18th September, 1947, I sailed from Liverpool."

Too often the commas are missed out. Sometimes the first comma only is inserted, and the omission of the second leaves the parenthesis open, as in: "On the 21st June, 1946 I sailed from Liverpool."

The second small matter I want to mention is the use of the comma before "Ltd.," the abbreviation for a limited company. Strictly, it is more correct to write "The X.Y. Jam Co., Ltd." than "The X.Y. Jam Co. Ltd., but the difference is unimportant, and my only advice is that you should be consistent. In any case, if you are writing for publication the point will most likely be decided by your editor, who in turn will be guided by his publisher's style-sheet.

WRONG USE OF THE COMMA

Many people have an irritating habit of separating a simple subject from its verb by a comma. I say "simple subject" for, as we have seen in the passage starting "Strong sense of dúty, . . ." (page 90), the last item of a compound subject might well take a comma before the verb.

A simple subject, however, is another matter, and you often find sentences of this kind: "My uncle and cousin, were going to the farm."

I cannot understand this error. Not only is the comma grammatically unjustified—it has no function for grouping or for parenthesis—but in speech there would be no pause before the verb. In the case of the compound subject, on the other hand, where the speaker would be reciting a catalogue of word-groups to make up his subject, there would be a pause before the verb.

Another common error is to misuse a comma in certain cases with a participle. Here are some examples:

"My guest, having gone home, I went to bed."

"Mr. B., being a little deaf, the speaker raised his voice."

These sentences, as written, are logically wrong. Each is a case of cause-and-effect grouping, the grouping being decided by the comma.

The subject of the first sentence is "I" and the subject of the second sentence is "the speaker." The other parts of the sentences, the groups dependent on the participles "having" and "being," are subordinate. The sentences should be punctuated thus:

"My guest having gone home, I went to bed."

"Mr. B. being a little deaf, the speaker raised his voice."

Now, the following sentences are quite all right:

"My guest, having gone home, arrived to find his house in darkness."

"Mr. B., being a little deaf, had to strain his ears to catch what the speaker said."

The subjects of the sentences are now "My guest" and "Mr.

B." The phrases "having gone home" and "being a little deaf" are now parenthetical, and are therefore put between pairs of commas.

Lastly, let me quote a notice I found in the bedroom of a London hotel:

"If you wish to stay beyond the period booked, it is essential, that, you contact reception office, on the evening before the original, departure date. Provided that, the room is still available, we will of course be pleased to help you. If not, we must hold you to the original booking."

There are, of course, far too many commas in this notice, and I prefer the word *notify* to the word *contact*. A better version of the same notice would be this:

"If you wish to stay beyond the period booked it is essential that you notify the reception office on the evening before the originally-planned departure date. Provided that the room is still available, we shall, of course, be pleased to help you. If the room is not available we must hold you to the original booking."

I am pleased about one thing in this notice. The writer has said "Provided that" instead of the much-misused "Providing that . . ." The present participle *providing* needs an attachment, such as the personal pronoun *I* in the following: "Providing the gardener with a spade, I asked him to dig the cabbage-patch."

ENUMERATION OF ADJECTIVES

If you have doubts about the use of the comma in the enumeration of adjectives, a safe and simple rule is this. If there are only two adjectives, omit the comma, as in "a hot dry day." If there are three or more adjectives in a row, use commas after all except the last, as in "a hot, dry, dusty day." You would write "a sticky sweet mixture" but "a sticky, sweet, warm, mysterious mixture."

With two adjectives you can use *and* if you wish, just as I have done in the previous paragraph—"a safe and simple rule."

THE USE OF THE COMMA WITH NUMERALS

Although it does not come within the sphere of grammar, the use of a comma with numerals should be mentioned briefly.

It is customary in the English-speaking world to divide a number into its thousands by the comma. Exceptions are dates (for example, 2000 B.C. and A.D. 1914) and reference numbers (for example, Model No. 3652).

Some publishers and printers, however, have a peculiar rule about this. If a four-figure number is followed by a decimal fraction, they say, the comma is omitted after the thousand group. Thus, while they would print 4,587, they would not print 4,587.85 but 4587.85.

It is interesting that while we use the comma to divide the thousands and the full-stop for the decimal point (85,617.23), Continental practice is the opposite (85.617,23).

THE COMMA WITH QUOTATIONS

The comma can be used to introduce quoted speeches, as in:

"As George entered the lounge with Tom he said, 'It's a good thing we booked early.' "

The colon can be used as an alternative, and this is dealt with more fully on page 100.

If a quotation is broken, however, commas must be used, as in the following:

" 'Before you go,' said my host, 'you must see my pictures.' "

A STRANGE PRESS CUSTOM

I have never discovered the reason for the popular Press custom of omitting the comma in such passages as these:

"Good not evil will result from his action."

"The Air Ministry forecasts a dry not wet day."

"I found that my uncle not my aunt was responsible." In each of these cases there should be a comma before "not." In the first two, there should be commas after "evil" and "wet," and in the third there should be a comma after "aunt."

THE SEMI-COLON

It is convenient to regard the semi-colon as something between the full-stop and the comma in value, though it is used much less frequently than either. It has a definite use, however—

for instance, when a slight break in a sentence is preferable to a new sentence.

The following are legitimate examples of the use of the semi-colon.

"The production from the illicit diggings surpasses by far that from the recognised mines; last year the company exported only £1,500,000 worth of diamonds, while the value of black-market exports is estimated at £10,000,000."

"The proposed extension to Malaysia would involve a capital of some millions of pounds; and we cannot help thinking of the lonely pioneer who eighty years ago arrived there with nothing."

"There is no mechanisation; the goods are made by skilled craftsmen who rejoice in the work of their hands."

"Some of his descriptions of natural scenery are very true and very pleasing in their simplicity; there is much tenderness and grace in his pastorals, but he never rises into passion."

"The idea of breaking down old European economic barriers is both bold and potentially fruitful; moreover it is now clear that it is practical."

THE SEMI-COLON IN VERSE

The semi-colon is much used in the writing of verse—and in verse I include everything from the highest level of true poetry to the meanest doggerel. In verse, a semi-colon is often used where a full-stop would be too abrupt and would tend to destroy the rhythm. Some poets like to use the colon, too, but often simply as a change from the semi-colon, from which it differs in value only slightly.

Shakespeare was fond of the semi-colon, but if I started giving examples of this fondness from the plays and poems I should never finish. If you open almost any book of verse you will see examples of the use of the semi-colon; the writing of verse, in fact, is good discipline in the grouping of words, and the punctuation of true poets is usually beyond reproach.

THE SEMI-COLON IN GROUPING

I alluded just now to the *grouping* of words, and the semi-colon is used where a stronger means of grouping is desirable than would be provided by the comma. Particularly is this the case in enumerations, where (as we have already seen) commas are not clear enough. An enumeration (or list) may be introduced by a colon, which is slightly stronger than a semi-colon and is useful for indicating that the writer is "leading up" to something. For an example of this use of the semi-colon you should refer to paragraph (b) on page 91.

WRONG USE OF THE SEMI-COLON

It is wrong to use a semi-colon where a comma should be used in the normal way. One fault which is not uncommon is to use a relative pronoun after such a misused semi-colon, as in the following sentences:

"We gave the chieftain a present of tobacco; which he accepted gratefully as if it were a handful of gold."

"Jonathan took his bride to a lonely island in the Outer Hebrides; where, it may be assumed, they were safe from the attentions of the Press."

"The Emperor in question was Napoleon Bonaparte; who, it will be conceded, had more than a spark of humanity."

In each of these sentences a comma should be used instead of the semi-colon.

In enumerations, semi-colons should be used only if commas would cause confusion, but they are often used in passages where commas would do. Here, for instance, is a list of adverse factors which have overtaken an unfortunate company:

"Dividends have been much reduced; the mines are among the deepest in the world; costs are likely to rise, and technical problems are increasing."

There is no justification for the semi-colons after the first two adverse factors. If the passage is intended to be read with a pause after each group of words the reader will use his own sense even if there are commas instead of semi-colons. In any case, if the writer of the sentence wanted to be consistent he should have used a semi-colon after the third item ("costs are likely to rise") instead of a comma.

Here is an extract from a newspaper's leading article:

"Having given his heirs all he dares; having bought the best advice on showing foresight; having taken every legal step to frustrate the tax-inspector, what prospect does the millionaire or the demi-millionaire face?"

The first two semi-colons are unnecessary. To be consistent in his malpractice, moreover, the writer should have used a semi-colon after "tax-inspector." The use of a comma here groups the final clause ("what prospect does the millionaire or the demi-millionaire face?") only with the last item of the enumeration ("having taken every legal step to frustrate the tax-inspector"), whereas the writer's intention is to group it with all the items.

The semi-colon has no right to be in the following:

"Summer temperatures, as one might suppose, reach unbearable heights, and the whole zone is one of utter desolation; no living thing, animal or vegetable existing there."

There should be a comma after "desolation" and another after "vegetable."

THE COLON

I have said that the colon is slightly stronger than the semi-colon. In the past, however, the two were used interchangeably, and either was used as an intermediate stop somewhere between the full-stop and comma in value. Many of the poets and dramatists had a liking for the colon, and in the Cathedral Psalter (the Prayer Book version of the Psalms) it was adopted as a symbol for the division of each verse into halves for chanting. The translators of the Bible liked both the colon and the semi-colon.

The use of the colon as a stop, or pause, has dwindled a great deal, but is not entirely dead. I think its most legitimate application, as a punctuation mark in the construction of a sentence, is to indicate that the part of the sentence which follows is a result of, or a direct corollary to, the preceding part.

Thus, in my opinion, the colon is more justified than the semi-colon in such a sentence as:

"Food was scarce in the forest that winter: neither of the woodmen had had any breakfast for three days."

A full-stop would have made two scrappy sentences. A semi-colon would have given the right rhythm, but would not have emphasised the connection between the two parts. A colon gives the strongest effect: the reader stops sharply on reaching it, and is forced to the reality of the situation by reading the subsequent part of the sentence.

Here is another good example of the justifiable use of the colon in punctuation:

"It is not a just law: in fact, it is unjust in the extreme."

THE COLON AS A LINK

I have referred to the colon as a *connecting* sign, and one very common use of it is not in the grammatical punctuation of a sentence but in connecting the general with the particular. This kind of construction is widespread and legitimate, with a phrase or a word following a sentence through a connecting colon:

"There are six rooms in the house: four upstairs and two downstairs."

"The explanation of his progress was to be found in one word: ambition."

"One of the first subjects to which the new Prime Minister will have to devote his attention is one to which the very structure of the Cabinet suggests a predisposition: European economic cooperation."

Now, in each of these cases a dash (—) would have served quite as well as a colon. There are, in fact, innumerable instances where the link between two items can be provided by either a dash or a colon.

In this book you will often find examples of writing introduced, perhaps, by the words "the following" and a colon, the colon being the link between the general and the particular. Sometimes I have used a dash and a colon.

THE COLON WITH QUOTATIONS

It is sometimes a practice to introduce any quoted material (words in quotation marks) by a colon. Where speech is concerned, however, too many colons can be conspicuous.

"As she stepped into the conservatory she saw a dark shape gliding over the floor. Involuntarily gasping: 'Oh!,' she went shivering into the commodious lounge and told her story to her horror-struck husband.

"He muttered: 'Come with me, my dear,' and led her into the library, where from a high shelf he took a dusty brown leather volume, smelling of age and mildew. Pointing to a chair, he said: 'Be seated. Listen to this.'

"For the first time in her life she listened to the dread story of the Fanshawes, and when the dry trembling recital came to an end two hours later she murmered: 'So that's it.' "

I think you will agree that the colons before the short speeches break up the prose too much. There is also a tendency to read the prose as if the colons were pauses. Commas could be used in place of the colons, and although they would not induce such mental hiatus they, too, might induce pauses where pauses were not intended.

My own practice in the case of such short speeches would be to ignore both colons and commas before the quotation marks and carry straight on, like this:

"Involuntarily gasping 'Oh!,' she went shivering into the commodious lounge. . . . He muttered 'Come with me, my dear.' . . . Pointing to a chair, he said 'Be seated. Listen to this.' . . . She murmered 'So that's it.' "

I use commas before somewhat longer quotations, and colons before still longer quotations. A single sentence, if not too long, may be preceded by a comma. A long sentence, or a passage of two or more sentences, may be preceded by a colon. Certainly, if a new paragraph is to start with a quotation, I introduce it by a colon.

THE COLON IN ABBREVIATIONS

There was once a practice of using a colon to indicate an abbreviation, just as today we use a full-stop. Occasionally you come across it even now, as in "No:," "Sept:," "Thurs:" and "Vol:." The only thing wrong with this practice is its obsolescence. The user may be faced, moreover, with the necessity of using a double colon, as in:

"This concession will apply to the following Nos:: 23, 64, 78."

THE QUESTION MARK

The question mark is not greatly maltreated, and on the whole literate people understand its use.

Unfortunately, however, it is too often omitted from those

requests which are politely given in the form of questions, such as, "Will you kindly note that I shall be away from home all next week?"

The writers of business correspondence are especially unconscious of the need for the question mark, especially if a question starts "Will you . . . ?" The following are examples of the requests that are sent out every day:

"Will you please return the plans at your convenience."

"Will you take steps to ensure that there is no recurrence of this trouble."

"Will you please supply the undermentioned goods." "May I . . . ?" is another beginning which, it is often assumed, does not need a question mark. It is not only Civil Servants who are guilty of writing like this:

"May I draw your attention to your non-compliance with the new condition embodied in Clause 32 (c)."

The assumption seems to be that where a question implies a command, an order, a request, there is no doubt about the answer. The writers of such sentences do not for a moment think that the readers may say "No." In spite of that, however, these sentences are grammatically in the form of questions, and therefore the question mark is absolutely necessary.

Fortunately for business and the rest of life, there are writers, even business men, who care about such niceties and who can be trusted to save English composition from decay.

THE QUESTION MARK: FURTHER NOTES

There are sentences which, though simple statements, are intended to imply questioning. In speech, the implication may be given by the tone of voice or the lilt, but in writing there is no logical justification for the question mark. Here are four examples:

"I wonder if I could see the manager."

"Surely it is not true."

"Don't tell me you are going away."

"You really haven't found it."

There is a strong temptation to use a question mark after such sentences as these, and although I shall not go so far as to say that you will be branded as illiterate if you use it, any sentence to justify the question mark should be framed as a question.

With the exception of the first example above, each sentence could be followed by an exclamation mark, as most probably it would be uttered in an exclamatory tone.

There are, moreover, exclamatory sentences which are expressed as questions but which do not take the question mark. "How are the mighty fallen!" is not a question but an oratorical way of saying "How the mighty are fallen!"

Such a construction can be either a question or an exclamation. Thus, "How often does it happen?" is a direct question. "How often does it happen!" is an exclamation of surprise at the frequency of "it."

There was a peculiar Victorian and Edwardian form of request starting with "Do you . . . ," which was not a question at all. These are two examples:

"Do you hold my horse while I look at his hoof."

"Do you take this road while I'll take that, and we'll see who arrives first."

In the first example, "Do you hold" was regarded as the imperative mood of the verb "to hold", and hence there was no hint of a question in this form of construction. "Do you take" was the imperative mood of the verb "to take."

One pitfall to be avoided is the use of a question mark in brackets after a word or phrase which you may consider unjustified. In readers' letters to newspapers this kind of facetiousness is not uncommon:

"The experience (?) of many of our city councillors should surely lead them to the conclusion that on new housing estates the roads should be laid first."

This, like a profusion of exclamation marks, is an unmistakable sign of the inexperienced writer. It amounts to a raising of the eyebrows, a nudge in the ribs. The writer is trying to imply that in his opinion many of the councillors lack experience, and he should boldly say so, even if it means another sentence. How, in speech, can a question mark be placed between two brackets?

THE EXCLAMATION MARK

With rare exceptions, the use of the exclamation mark must be limited to exclamations, exclamatory sentences and exclamatory phrases.

That is my rule. When I read one of my first articles in print, many years ago, I was horrified to find how foolish it looked. There was an exclamation mark after every few sentences. I am surprised now that the editor was so lenient, or so imperceptive, for, as I have said above, a profusion of exclamation marks is an unmistakable sign of the novice.

Thousands of people (especially the more demonstrative among us) are prone to this failing and exhibit it in their writings. These people seem incapable of writing personal letters without these emblems of emotion. They wrongly think that every sentence meant to be surprising, amusing, peculiar, or in any way out of the ordinary, should be followed by an exclamation mark.

"This is funny," they seem to say, or "This is witty, this is astonishing, this will make your hair curl." But the truth is that the essence of the surprise, the humour, the wit, the unusual, should be in the writing itself, and if these qualities are lacking all the exclamation marks in the whole world will not create them.

To return to my first paragraph, however, I have no doubt that you know what exclamations are. Another name for them is "interjections," which I described in Chapter III (page 34).

An exclamatory sentence could be something like this: "All my jewels have been stolen!" Such a statement looks too casual without the exclamation mark, as if the speaker did not care very much. Other examples are:

"He surely hasn't come home already!"

"I am saved at last!" "Get out!"

A point to remember is that exclamatory sentences are usually *quoted* sentences spoken emotionally or under stress. A passage in narrative form would certainly *not* be written like this:

"She entered the room and found that all her jewels had been stolen! Her black-sheep brother surely had not come home already! Then she remembered that her brother had just been elected to the city council, and had decided to reform. Clearly he could not have been the culprit. He was saved at last! She need not tell him to get out!"

Exclamatory phrases are such observations as "Goodness me!", "Upon my word!", "What a mess!", and "Oh! What a beautiful morning!"

Even more horrible than the unrestrained use of single exclamation marks is the very common vice of using them in pairs or in threes. It is as if the writer is screaming at his reader to take special notice of his devastating sentence, but the civilised writer should not adopt the tactics of the signwriter or the poster artist.

The general attitude to the exclamation mark is the attitude of the naïve minister in Barrie's *Farewell, Miss Julie Logan*. The Rev. Adam Yestreen is explaining humour to Miss Julie.

"I drew a note of exclamation, and showed her how they were put into books, at the end of sentences, to indicate that the remark was of a humorous character. She got the loan of the pencil and practised making notes of exclamation under my instruction."

QUOTATION MARKS

First, let me say that the term "quotation marks" is far better than the old-fashioned "inverted commas." For one thing, only the first marks (")—before the quotation—are inverted commas, the second marks (") being commas the right way round but stuck up in the air.

For another thing, the term "inverted commas" is top-heavy. And for another (even though this is a book on English), French quotation marks are not commas, inverted or otherwise, but are like this: « ».

Then let us consider what quotation marks are for. Primarily, they are for anything *actually quoted*; this may sound silly, but, as you will see later, it is not as silly as it sounds. Quotation marks are for quoting speech, or for copying something that is written. They are for illustrating the unusualness, doubtfulness, or other peculiarity, real or imagined, of a word or a group of words. They may be used for titles of books, plays, films, articles, poems and periodicals, and for names of ships, paintings, houses, inns and hotels.

SINGLE AND DOUBLE QUOTATION MARKS

Many people are understandably confused by the apparently indiscriminate use of single quotation marks (' ') and double quotation marks (" ").

D*

The more logical practice is to use single marks for all quotations unless there is one quotation inside another, when the inside quotation receives double marks. This practice gives this kind of result:

'As I walked out of the house I said to him, "We shall never meet again." Yet, had I known it, I was wrong.'

'The title of the book, "Purple Skies," gives no clue as to its contents.'

'The dictatorial policy of "indoctrination" has proved futile.'

For some reason which nobody can explain, however, conventional practice in this direction is illogical. It is more conventional to use double marks for all quoted matter except for quoted quotations, which are given single marks. The practice of using single marks inside double marks is the practice I am adopting throughout this book. Some publishers like it the other way—as in the examples above—and in writing for publication you may be governed by the publisher's style.

MISUSE OF QUOTATION MARKS

It is important to remember that quotation marks enclose passages which are *actually quoted*. Writers who have failed in the observance of this obvious truth, thereby displaying illogical minds, include novelists whose pages abound with passages in quotation marks which are not quotations at all.

Let me show what I mean by a simple example:

"Jack Horner said, 'What a good boy am I!'"

The double quotation marks, incidentally, show that the passage is merely an example, and not part of the text of the book.

The speech "What a good boy am I!" consists of Jack's *actual words*, and is thus a quotation. (Notice the correct use of the exclamation mark.)

But if the sentence had been expressed in this way: "Jack said that he was a good boy," the actual words are not given. Hence there is no quotation, and the use of quotation marks would be wrong.

Yet, in effect, many novelists and other kinds of writers would write the second example thus:

"Jack said that 'he had been a good boy.'" You will realise that this is entirely wrong.

LITERARY EXAMPLES

Jane Austen had an irritating trick of putting in quotation marks passages in which the speaker was referred as to *he* instead of *I*. Look at this, from *Persuasion,* where Sir Walter is addressing a company:

"Sir Walter thought much of Mrs. Wallis; she was said to be an excessively pretty woman, beautiful. 'He longed to see her. He hoped she might make some amends for the many very plain faces he was continually passing in the streets. . . . It was evident how little the women were used to the sight of anything tolerable, by the effect which a man of decent appearance produced. . . .' Modest Sir Walter!"

The words in the single quotation marks are obviously not the words Sir Walter used, for the speaker would have used *I* and the present tense of the verbs. As the passage is written, the quotation marks are wrong and unnecessary.

Here is another example from the same novel:

"A knock at the door suspended every thing. 'A knock at the door! and so late! . . . . Mrs. Clay decidedly thought it Mr. Elliot's knock.' Mrs. Clay was right."

Presumably Mrs. Clay was speaking; but why did Jane Austen use quotation marks when she was not giving Mrs. Clay's actual words?

Towards our own time, even such celebrated novelists as Sir Hugh Walpole have not been guiltless. Consider this, from *The Secret City*:

"He would tell you, if you inquired, that 'he couldn't stand those fellows who looked into every glass they passed.'"

If Walpole had wanted to give the man's speech in quotation marks, it would probably have been like this:

" 'I can't stand those fellows who look into every glass they pass.' "

The alternative form would be as it is printed, but without the quotation marks, thus:

"He would tell you, if you inquired, that he couldn't stand those fellows who looked into every glass they passed."

Here is an extract from an erstwhile advertisement of an oil company:

"Forty-six years ago Blériot flew the Channel and in the

prophetic words of Lord Northcliffe at the time 'Britain was no longer an island.' "

The words of Lord Northcliffe were "Britain is no longer an island," and the error of the copywriter is emphasised by the phrase "at the time."

The passage, in fact, is slightly confused. The copywriter probably wanted to use the phrase "prophetic words," and realised that this called for a quotation. "Britain is" would not have sounded right in association with "Blériot flew," and therefore "Britain was" appeared.

Reconstruction would have solved the problem, in some such manner as the following:

"Forty-six years ago Blériot flew the Channel, and, as Lord Northcliffe remarked at the time, Britain was no longer an island."

QUOTATION MARKS WITH FULL-STOPS AND COMMAS

You have probably noticed that in most newspapers, and in some books and magazines, closing quotation marks are placed *after* a full-stop or comma if there happens to be one.

This is done purely for appearance, even if the full-stop or comma is not part of the quotation. I think you will probably agree that, of the following examples, the first of each pair looks neater on the page:

" 'My name is Samuel,' he said."
" 'My name is Samuel', he said."
"His address is 'Sunniside,' King's Road."
"His address is 'Sunniside', King's Road."

Logically, however, the comma in each of these is not part of the quotation, and should be outside the closing mark. Usually, in fact, the logical place for a comma *is* outside. An exception can occur in an interrupted speech of which the comma forms a part, as in:

" 'There are, unfortunately,' she said, 'very few first-class applicants for the post.' "

The comma after "unfortunately" is part of the broken sentence, is therefore part of the quotation, and correctly appears before the intermediate quotation mark.

In the following example the comma is *not* part of the broken sentence, and correctly appears after the intermediate quotation mark:

" 'There are', she said, 'very few first-class applicants.' " Yet according to convention this would be printed thus:

" 'There are,' she said, 'very few first-class applicants.' "

If we want to follow logic, a full-stop can be placed inside or outside, the position depending on the mental sequence. In the following examples, the full-stop is rightly placed outside:

"Lady Nugent, as we have seen, could not paint her flamingo, but had to call in 'a nature artist'."

"Lack of sunlight, shortages of fresh fruit and vegetables and the intense cold combine to bring on what is called 'Lapp sickness'."

(This sentence would be better with commas after *vegetables* and *cold*. And *so-called* would be better than *what is called*.)

"Above all, Griffo supplied a novel fount . . . . based on the 'cancelleresca corsiva' of the papal chancery, which humanists had taken over for their informal writing, and later received the name of 'italics'."

If you are writing for publication, you will probably, in this matter, be in the hands of your publisher, who will adhere to his house style. Unfortunately some publishers go to the extreme of an illogical style and always place the full-stops outside the quotation marks. This can lead to absurd results, as in the following examples:

"To Charles XII these occupations of Peter afforded some scornful amusement. 'Let him build towns' are the words accredited to him 'and we will come and take them'."

" 'One ambassador flies out as another flies in'."

"When Dr. Johnson averred that Milton's *Lycidas* was *easy*, *vulgar* and therefore *disgusting*, he intended to say that it was 'effortless, popular, and therefore not in good taste'."

Generally, however, the convention of the majority of publishers and printers—that is, in placing closing quotation marks outside full-stops and commas—has much to commend it. It avoids inconsistency, and it gives a balanced appearance to manuscript, typescript and printing.

QUOTATION MARKS WITH OTHER PUNCTUATION MARKS

When it comes to the use of quotation marks with punctuation marks other than the full-stop and the comma, logic seems to be the only guide. Let us consider, in turn, the semi-colon, the colon, the question mark and the exclamation mark, which are the only punctuation marks affected.

The Semi-colon

The semi-colon can easily come after a quotation or after a word in quotation marks, as in the following:

"He unfurled the banner bearing the magic word 'Excelsior'; then, at the head of his little band, he marched proudly into the night."

The semi-colon, by virtue of its nature, can hardly come at the end of, and inside, a quotation.

The Colon

The colon, too, can come after a quotation, as in this example:

"The following is the cast of 'Macbeth': ...."

The Question Mark

The question mark can be inside, outside, or both. Here are three examples, one of each kind of application:

"Are you happy?"

"Did you see 'The Maid of Orleans'?"

"Did she say 'Do you love me?'?"

Marguerite Steen, in *Twilight on the Floods*, has misplaced a question mark in the following:

"Yet how could he say bluntly: 'I have married the girl you love?'"

This should be:

"Yet how could he say bluntly: 'I have married the girl you love.'?"

The Exclamation Mark

The exclamation mark, like the question mark, can be in three positions:

" 'Get out of my sight!' he said."

"How horrid of him to call you 'Parasite'!"

"How casual of him just to say 'Oh!'!"

INTERRUPTED QUOTATIONS

I have already dealt with interrupted speeches of this
kind:

"'It's all right,' he gasped with relief, 'there's nobody
in.'"

But another kind of interruption in a quotation or an extract
is an interpolation, or explanatory note put in by the quoter
for the benefit of the reader. Sometimes you see such inter-
polations enclosed by ordinary brackets, but this method is
clearly inadequate as the quotation itself may contain words
in such brackets.

One convention in printing is the use of square brackets to
distinguish the interpolation from words in ordinary round
brackets forming part of the quotation. Here is an example of
such practice:

"The Member for South Beasley said: 'The Minister has
pointed out that when the Imported Inks (Restriction of
Colours) Bill becomes law, it [the Bill] will not seek to prohibit
ink-users from selecting their favourite colours when purchasing
inks. Can the Minister give us his assurance that when they
[inks] are bought, they will be found to be equal in quality and
in the fastness of their dyes with the inks at present obtain-
able?' (Laughter.)"

The square brackets indicate that the words they enclose
are not part of the speech of the Member for South Beasley, but
are simply inserted to help the reader to define "it" and "they."
All typewriter keyboards do not include square brackets, however, and personally I like to break the quotation or the extract
with quotation marks and dashes. The square-bracketed parts
of the above would then appear in this way:

"'. . . . Bill becomes law, it'—the Bill—'will not seek to
prohibit . . . . that when they'—inks—'are bought, they will be
found . . .'"

QUOTATION MARKS WITH PARAGRAPHS

When a quoted passage or speech is divided into paragraphs,
it is customary to use quotation marks at the beginning of the
passage and at the beginning of each paragraph, but only the
last paragraph is given quotation marks at the end.

MULTI-LINE QUOTATIONS

Multi-line quotations are the name I give, in default of a better name, to those quotations which, occupying two or more lines of manuscript or type, are given quotation marks at the beginning of each line. This absurd cult looks hideous, and I was pleased when *The Guardian* (formerly *The Manchester Guardian*), one of its last strongholds, abandoned it. The practice could perhaps be excused if it could be justified, but there is nothing whatever to recommend it.

If the object is to distinguish a lengthy quotation from the rest of the text, it would be better achieved by offsetting the margin of the quotation from the margin of the text.

CHAPTER VIII

More Punctuation

W̲E̲ are not yet finished with punctuation. You are perhaps realising by now that it is a far bigger and more important subject than you thought, as well as being quite fascinating. We are a little more than half-way in our study, and when we come to the end I hope you will see that good punctuation is a sign of a clear mind.

THE HYPHEN

The hyphen, a really logical punctuation mark, is not used as much as it should be. It has two functions. One is to link separate words to make one "compound word." The other is to act as a grouping agent, that is, to link words in a sentence to preserve the sense intended by the writer.

COMPOUND WORDS

A table is one object, and a lamp is another. A table-lamp is not only a special kind of lamp but is a third object, the word being composed of two nouns. If *table* had been an adjective no hyphen would have been required, and hence we have *electric lamp* without the hyphen.

If the first part of the compound word can be either noun or adjective, it is safer to use a hyphen if the lack of a hyphen would give an absurd result. Thus, a *salt cellar* is strictly a cellar made of salt, but there is no mistaking a *salt-cellar*. A *wood stove* may be interpreted as a stove made of wood, and so we write *wood-stove* and *oil-stove*. The choice of *iron ore* or *iron-ore* depends on one's preference for treating *iron* as an adjective or a noun; scientifically, it should be *iron-ore*.

A *writing desk* would be an unusually talented desk, but a *writing-desk* is an ordinary piece of furniture. A *walking stick* and *stepping stones* must be magical, but a *walking-stick* and *stepping-stones* are understandable.

Other compound words in which the hyphen makes all the difference between sense and nonsense include the following: *soap-box, copper-miner, pork-butcher, laughing-gas, cloth-brush, paper-fastener, changing-room.*

There has always been a tendency to drop the hyphen where desirable and unite the two words into one after the combination has been generally accepted, and today we have *lampshade, inkwell, nightdress, washbowl, haystack, postgraduate, earthworks* and *wayleave.* I like this tendency, except when it produces such awkward combinations as *earring.*

THE HYPHEN AS A GROUPING AGENT

We saw on page 84 in Chapter VI that compound adjectives require the hyphen. Examples I gave there included *face-saving action, newly-married couple* and *public-spirited council.*

Of these examples, *face-saving* and *public-spirited* are always adjectives. The hyphen is thus still necessary if we write: "His action was face-saving" or "The council was public-spirited."

Newly married, however, need not be a compound adjective but simply a pair of independent words, so that if we write "They are newly married" the hyphen is not needed.

Similar examples are provided by the following pairs of sentences:

"The day was never to be forgotten."	"It was a never-to-be-forgotten day."
"The privilege is greatly abused."	"It is a greatly-abused privilege."
"She is well dressed."	"She is a well-dressed woman."
"The circuit is rated at 250 volts."	"It is a 250-volt circuit."
"The pump delivery is two inches in diameter."	"The pump has a two-inch delivery."

In the last two examples you will notice the change from plural to singular when the quantitative words are compounded into adjectives. Similarly we should write of "a six-man committee," not "a six-men committee."

The use of the hyphen in compound adjectives is not as widespread as it should be, even in places where it might be expected. Notorious examples are provided in the names of Government Bills and Acts, such as the Defence of the Realm Act, but fortunately there is a suggestion of grouping in the use of capital initial letters, which may vindicate the Parliamentary draftsmen.

DOUBLE COMPOUND ADJECTIVES

What is a writer to do with a compound adjective made up of (*a*) two compound adjectives or (*b*) one compound adjective and one single adjective? Slovenly thought in this direction can lead to such graceless grouping as the following:

1. "The United Kingdom-United States agreement."
2. "The Jane Smith-Harold Jones wedding."
3. "The Great Yarmouth-London road."
4. "The Southern-Great Western joint branch."
5. "South African-born Indians."
6. "Conservative-National Liberal alliance."
7. "Dirty oil-remover."

These examples really call for another punctuation mark which is, in fact, used by some printers. This mark is longer than a hyphen and shorter than a dash, but it is not in general use and it is not on the keyboard of any typewriter I know. In manuscript it would be especially difficult to differentiate between it and the hyphen and the dash.

This long hyphen (if we call it that) would be placed between the two parts of a double compound adjective, and the words of each part (if more than one) would be linked by an ordinary hyphen.

I feel that there are already enough punctuation marks, however, and to invent new ones would add to the confusion. It is better to do the best we can with the hyphen, and I should write or type the foregoing phrases thus:

1. "The United-Kingdom-United-States agreement."
2. "The Jane-Smith-Harold-Jones wedding."
3. "The Great-Yarmoutn-London road."
4. "The Southern-Great-Western joint branch."

5. "South-African-born Indians."
6. "Conservative-National-Liberal alliance."
7. "Dirty-oil-remover."

Two oil companies, the Shell Company and the Royal Dutch Company, do a great deal of work in common under the joint name of a group. Quite often the activities of the group are reported in the Press, but there seems to be no agreed and satisfactory manner of writing the name of the group. I have seen "Royal Dutch-Shell Group," "Royal Dutch/Shell Group" and "Royal-Dutch Shell Group."

The first is blatantly wrong, and the second uses the oblique stroke which puts the practice in the horrible "and/or" category. The third is the least offensive, but does not make any attempt to symbolise the connection between the two companies. "Royal-Dutch-Shell Group" would be the most logical way of writing, but quite a satisfactory way out of the difficulty is to omit the hyphens and write simply "Royal Dutch Shell Group," which offends nobody.

WORDS WITH PREFIXES

The subject of prefixes arises out of the business of grouping, but here I must make a short digression.

A prefix is something placed *before* a word to modify the meaning. The following is a list of prefixes in common use:

pre- (before)	*supra-* (above)
ante- (before)	*super-* (above)
post- (after)	*infra-* (below)
anti- (against)	*ex-* (former)
pro- (for)	*ex-* (out of)
contra- (against, opposite to)	*ultra-* (more than)

My reason for this digression is simply that sometimes, but not always, the prefix is linked with the main word by a hyphen. There seems to be no law determining which words are to have the hyphen, but most probably all the words with prefixes originally had hyphens which have been discarded by general and tacit agreement in the course of time.

Thus, today we have *prehistoric* but *pre-Christian*, *predecease* but *pre-determine*, *antediluvian* but (sometimes) *ante-dated*, *post-prandial* but *posthumous*.

We have *antipathetic* but *anti-national, anticlimax* but *anti-revolutionary, proportional* but *pro-British*.

Most of the *contra-, supra-* and *super-* words are written without the hyphen, examples being *contradict, supranational, supernatural. Infra-red* and *ultra-violet* are written with or without the hyphen. *Ex-* is usually given the hyphen.

When a prefix is linked by a hyphen with a proper name, it is usual to start the prefix with a small letter even though the proper name starts with a capital. Examples included in the foregoing lists are *pre-Christian* and *pro-British*. A compound adjective which has become independent of the main word, however, is the geological name *Precambrian*, which logically should be *pre-Cambrian*.

Be careful how you use hyphened prefixes with double words. For example, think how absurd are written expressions (often seen in the Press) like these:

"Mr. A., the ex-Home Secretary, was at the reception."

"In spite of his anti-trade union attitude, Lord X. is a militant champion of the masses."

"Before becoming pro-Free Churches, the Bishop of X. was a staunch High Anglican."

"Ex-Home-Secretary" would look peculiar, but why not use "former Home Secretary"? "Anti-trade-union" is all right, as it is a compound adjective preceding a noun. "Pro-Free-Churches" is not satisfactory, and here some reconstruction is necessary. I should write: "Before becoming a supporter of Free Churches, the Bishop of X. was a staunch High Anglican."

EFFECT OF THE OMISSION OF THE HYPHEN

We have already seen some of the queer effects that can be produced by the omission of the hyphen, as in *wood stove, writing desk* and *walking stick*. In an old newspaper I have been reading of the effect of petrol-rationing on "small business heads" (instead of "small-business heads").

What about the headline, "Man Eating Tiger in Zoo"? The omission of the hyphen between *man* and *eating* is a comical mistake, but it is by no means rare.

A vapour-lamp is advertised as "producing a germ destroying vapour." Literally interpreted, this means that the lamp produces a germ which destroys vapour. All that is needed to give the right sense is a hyphen in "germ-destroying."

I have also read of a "French polisher." As it stands, this means a polisher of French nationality, but if the reference is to a man who does French polishing he should be described as a "French-polisher."

THE HYPHEN: MISCELLANEOUS NOTES

I have explained the justification for the hyphen in words like *copper-miner*. Similarly, the hyphen is necessary in the following words and all others like them, even if there is no following noun as in *man-eating tiger*:

copper-mining	*steel-production*	*tool-making*
coal-mining	*gas-manufacture*	*house-hunting*
tea-planting	*novel-writing*	*portrait-painting*

It should be noted that words like *nickel plating* are *not* in this category, as *nickel* is an adjective and the *plating* is not done on the nickel but on the underlying metal. *Nickel-plating* would imply that the nickel itself was plated. *Tin plate* does not normally need a hyphen, but the accepted term is *tinplate*.

We may have an enumeration of hyphenated words, as in the sentence: "He is interested in gold-mining, silver-mining and copper-mining." If we wanted to write this as it would probably be said, we should be perfectly justified in writing: "He is interested in gold-, silver- and copper-mining."

There is no justification for the hyphen in *today* and *tomorrow*, and I am glad to see that more and more publishers are growing enlightened in this respect. Who would think of writing *yester-day*?

If *good-bye* genuinely consisted of two words the hyphen might be justified. But as it is a corruption of "God be with you!" it might just as well be written *goodbye*.

Two awkward words are *cooperate* and *coordinate*, with their derivatives *cooperation*, *cooperative* and *coordination*. It is generally accepted that the hyphen is no more justified in these words than it is in other *co-* words—*coagulate*, *coincidence*, *cosine*, *cotangent*. The hyphen may be used to avoid any suggestion of an *oo* sound, but it also produces anomalies like *unco-ordinated* and *unco-operative*.

The Americans have got over the difficulty by using a "diaeresis"—two dots over the second of a pair of adjacent vowels to indicate a change in vowel sound—which results in *coöperate* and *coördinate*. But I do not care for this as the diaeresis is not a truly English device and is awkward in writing and typing. Personally I simply use *cooperate* and *coordinate*, and anyone should know better than to read an *oo* sound into them.

I wish the Press would give up their queer convention of hyphenating street-names. I have never yet discovered the origin of this unjustified and illogical practice, which results, for instance, in the following: *St. James's-st.*, *Piccadilly-circus*, *Tottenham Court-rd.*, *Kensington-gdns.* and *Whitehall-cres.*

I think that is all I need say about the hyphen. I should add, however, that, while it is important to use it where it is justified, the hyphen should not be used unnecessarily. The use of too many hyphens is nearly as bad as the use of too few.

OTHER MEANS OF ADJECTIVAL GROUPING

By "adjectival grouping" I simply mean the grouping of two or more words to form a compound adjective, as in "six-man committee" and "North-Atlantic-Treaty-Organisation countries."

We have seen that the usual method of grouping is by means of the hyphen. There are, however, two other ways which I must mention.

If the group of words forming the adjective happens to be in quotation marks for one reason or another, hyphens are superfluous. Suitable examples are in the following sentences:

"The extraordinary meeting of the council resulted in the formation of a special 'coordination of committees' plan."

"For the purpose of attracting tourists it was decided to inaugurate a 'Welcome to Dulltown' campaign."

"The magnificent 'Daily Drummer' trophy was won by Mrs. Queetch."

In the last example, "Daily Drummer" might have been printed in *italics*, as is the custom of some publishers, but in such cases there are no quotation marks. The use of italics, in fact, is the other method of grouping without the hyphen, and in writing or typing it is customary to underline any words which are to be set in italics.

Foreign phrases are usually printed in italics, and when they are used as adjectives it is not necessary to use the hyphen. We need not write "*bona-fide* claim" as the italics in "*bona fide* claim" provide sufficient grouping. Similarly, we should write "*à la carte* menu" and "*hors de combat* army."

There might even be a third system of grouping where omission of the hyphen is justified. I have referred to the "North-Atlantic-Treaty-Organisation countries." In practice, of course, the hyphens never appear in this grouping, and the Press may be justified in regarding the four words as a well-known group in themselves without any further aid, especially when each word is started with a capital letter. The capital initials, in fact, are frequently regarded as self-sufficient, and the organisation has developed into "N.A.T.O.," with or without the full-stops.

THE DASH

To many people, the dash (—) is the only punctuation mark known. They scatter dashes freely about their correspondence, to take the place of full-stops, commas, colons and semi-colons. If they do permit themselves a little relaxation from this dull practice it is probably only to use the double or treble exclamation mark.

The dash has three main functions—as a pause, as an indication of parenthesis, and as a link.

THE DASH AS A PAUSE

When a dash is used to indicate a pause in a sentence, it is essential that after the pause the continuation is strongly linked with the part of the sentence preceding the dash. The reader or listener must *expect* something to follow the pause. In speech this expectation could be induced by the speaker's intonation, but in writing the best means of indication is the dash.

The following are typical examples of this function of the dash:

"It was not a lion—it was a tiger, furiously lashing its way through the undergrowth."

"That season Farmer Montgomery helped with my harvest—not before time, I thought."

"In agriculture the colony is quite advanced—far ahead, in

fact, of either of the neighbouring colonies, which are still using primitive methods of irrigation."

The following is a *bad* example of this function of the dash:

"It will be for the Council to decide whether the property after improvement or conversion will have a useful life which will justify the spending of public money on it—the law requires that the expected life must be more than fifteen years."

It would have been better if a full-stop had taken the place of the dash and a new sentence started with "The law . . ."

THE DASH IN PARENTHESIS

The second function of the dash is parenthetical, and of course two dashes are required to give the parenthesis. (You should refer for a moment to Chapter VI, page 77.) A pair of dashes may be equivalent to a pair of brackets or a pair of commas, but not always. Consider the following sentence:

"All night long they toiled—it was their third night without sleep—and by morning they were completely exhausted."

Here, commas could not properly be used. Brackets could be used with the same effect as dashes:

"All night long they toiled (it was their third night without sleep) and by morning they were completely exhausted."

I think so much is generally understood. But often you find that a writer—even in print—will start a parenthesis with a dash and then forget to finish it. Such lapses can lead to this kind of writing:

"The Mayor's annual banquet—at which His Worship the Mayor, the Mayoress, the Sheriff, the Aldermen, the Councillors, and several visiting notabilities were present, was held today at the Town Hall."

Having chosen a dash to open his parenthesis the writer must use a dash to close it, and the right place for it in the above sentence is between *present* and *was*. If the writer had started with a bracket he would probably have noticed the need for a bracket at the other end.

Commas could have been used in this sentence instead of dashes or brackets, but the parenthesis is so long that the reader might have become confused. I now suggest that you refer to the sections, "Commas in Enumeration," page 89, and "Parenthetical Use of Commas," page 91.

An interesting point arises when dashes or brackets are used with a legitimate comma. Consider the sentence:

"Harps are expensive, and harpists are scarce." The comma after *expensive* is justified.

Now, suppose that the writer wishes to interpolate in parenthesis some information about harps—for example, "a good harp costs well over a thousand pounds."

The most suitable place to put it is after *expensive*, so that the sentence takes either of the following forms:

"Harps are expensive—a good harp costs well over a thousand pounds—, and harpists are scarce."

"Harps are expensive (a good harp costs well over a thousand pounds), and harpists are scarce."

Now, although the comma after the second bracket looks all right, the comma after the second dash looks out of place. Actually, it is not out of place at all, and logically it should be there. For some reason which I cannot explain, however, or perhaps for no reason whatever, parenthetical dashes are nowadays regarded as having the power of absorbing the second comma, or doing its job for it. In other words, the second dash fulfils the joint functions of a dash and a comma.

It was not always so, and in writings published before the early part of the twentieth century you will find that the comma in such cases is fully recognised and inserted. Today it rarely is.

THE DASH AS A LINK

The third use of the dash is to indicate a connecting link between the general and the particular. I have dealt with this on page 100 ("The Colon as a Link"), and in this book there are several places where I have introduced examples with the dash, usually in conjunction with the colon. Thus, on page 18, you will find:

"The following are the parts of speech:—"

BRACKETS

The use of brackets to indicate parenthesis has already been dealt with in Chapter VI (under "Parenthesis") and in my foregoing section on dashes. I have therefore little further to say about brackets: their use is only parenthetical, they are always in pairs, and a bracket by itself has no reason for existence.

You should be careful when a closing bracket comes at the end of a sentence, a clause, or a phrase, in such a way that it is next to a full-stop or a comma. Often, too often, you see mistakes in the order of punctuation, and the following examples are all wrong:

"The 5.30 will stop at Sheffield (Midland) and Leeds (City.)"

"The film is called 'To Shape Tomorrow.' (Subject: Plastics)."

"I thank you for your letter of the 15th and have pleasure in returning your plan (of which, incidentally, I have made a copy.)"

The comma seems to be less vulnerable than the full-stop when used beside a closing bracket, but I have seen punctuation like this:

"He showed me his bicycle (a very nice bicycle,) and let me have a ride."

The correct versions of the above four sentences are:

"The 5.30 will stop at Sheffield (Midland) and Leeds (City)."

"The film is called 'To Shape Tomorrow' (subject: Plastics)." *Alternative*: "The film is called 'To Shape Tomorrow.' (Subject: Plastics.)"

"I thank you for your letter of the 15th and have pleasure in returning your plan (of which, incidentally, I have made a copy)."

"He showed me his bicycle (a very nice bicycle), and let me have a ride."

Strictly, the writer of the third example should not have used brackets, as the second part of his sentence is a relative clause rather than a parenthesis. The following would have been preferable:

"I thank you for your letter of the 15th, and have pleasure in returning your plan, of which, incidentally, I have made a copy."

SQUARE BRACKETS

While ordinary round brackets have their place in the course of a written sentence, and in fact are part of a written sentence, square brackets—[ ]—are generally used to enclose something that is put in, perhaps by way of explanation, but is not part of the sentence. (See also page 111.)

If you look at page 73, Chapter VI, in the section on "Longer Sentences," you will see what I mean.

"I live [*verb*] in a house."

The explanatory word *verb* is obviously not part of the sentence, and thus has to be distinguished somehow from the words of the sentence, "I live in a house,"

If round brackets were used, it would mean that the word *verb*, in parenthesis, was part of the sentence. To show its independence from the words of the sentence, therefore, it is enclosed in square brackets.

A common example of the use of square brackets is the interpolation of something into a quotation—the interpolation of a word or phrase which is not actually part of the quotation. The following example is from a book review:

"According to the author's preface, 'the book was planned to give the nation some idea of the conditions under which they [the pygmies] lived in the early nineteenth century.' If he has not succeeded, it is not his fault."

The words *the pygmies* are an explanatory note inserted by the reviewer. Round brackets would have made the words part of the quotation, but as they are not part of the quotation they are enclosed in square brackets.

I prefer to do it this way—by breaking the quotation and using a pair of dashes:

"According to the author's preface, 'the book was planned to give the nation some idea of the conditions under which they'—the pygmies—'lived in the early nineteenth century.' . . ."

THE APOSTROPHE

The apostrophe is used to indicate possession, and I have written about this in Chapter II (page 21). In that chapter I have explained when you should use apostrophe-*s* ('*s*) and *s*-apostrophe (*s*'). Since writing that, however, I have come across a Press reference to "the Dean of St. Paul's note."

There is something wrong here, of course, but admittedly the case is unusual. If "the Dean of St. Paul's" is the recognised title, what is the corresponding construction to "the King of Spain's beard," "the Archbishop of Canterbury's speech" and "the Duke of Norfolk's privilege"?

If we write "the Dean of St. Paul's's note" it looks queer and it sounds queer if spoken. I am not sure if we can forgive the newspaper for printing "The Dean of St. Paul's note," and the best way out of the difficulty would be to write "the note of the Dean of St. Paul's."

The apostrophe is also used in abbreviations like *shouldn't, can't, isn't, I'd, he's, we'll, they're*. Two peculiar abbreviations are *won't* and *shan't*. *Won't* means *will not*, and the only explanation I can give for the strange form of abbreviation is that it rhymes with *don't*.

Shan't, meaning *shall not*, should have two apostrophes, and in many nineteenth-century books it is written as *sha'n't*. For many years now, however, the first apostrophe has been discarded.

Then there are words like *'bus* and *'phone*. These started as definite abbreviations, but the apostrophe has either been dropped or is gradually being dropped as the abbreviated forms are accepted into the language as true words. *Bus* and *phone* have now become as legitimate as *pram*.

MARKS OF OMISSION

It is often necessary to copy an extract from something—from a report, an article, a book, a letter, or a speech. In the course of the extract you probably find that everything is not relevant to your present purpose, and that certain parts, having nothing to do with that purpose, can be omitted. What are you to do to avoid tedium for the copyist and the reader?

The customary way of showing that something has been omitted from a quotation is by means of a row of three or four dots, not too closely spaced. If the end of a sentence falls immediately before the omission, the full-stop should be shown in its proper place. If the omission starts in the middle of a sentence, a space must be left between the last word and the first dot. I shall give an example showing both kinds of omission:

Original version

"The Minister said that it had always been his aim to assist small shopkeepers. A large number of small purchases in a populous area could give a substantial turnover, but agricultural areas were less fortunate. Subsidies of the kind suggested by the Hon. Member would relieve hardship, but at the same time might tend to promote a certain lethargy. It was not his intention to set up a Royal Commission, but the Ministry would investigate any special claims of outstanding merit."

Abbreviated version

"The Minister said that it had always been his aim to assist small shopkeepers. . . . Subsidies of the kind suggested . . . might tend to promote a certain lethargy. . . . The Ministry would investigate any special claims of outstanding merit."

Dots can also be used at the end of a quoted passage to show that the quotation is incomplete.

The use of dots is a device, too, of some novelists, to indicate perhaps a pause or an incomplete speech. Often, however, they are used for no particular reason, and can be misleading.

CAPITAL LETTERS

I consider that capital letters, being in a way a guide to the reader, can be included in a study of punctuation.

Far too many people use initial capital letters indiscriminately, not only in their personal correspondence but also in official, commercial and technical writing. I could fill a chapter with the use and misuse of capital letters, but instead I shall deal with a few important or interesting practices.

I shall say little about the use of a capital letter at the start of a sentence, as it is evident that everybody adopts this practice. I should remind you, however, that you must not start a sentence with a numeral. I have just seen this reader's letter to a newspaper: "£9 is barely sufficient to buy . . . ." This should have been sub-edited to: "Nine pounds is barely sufficient . . . ."

The use of capitals for proper names, and for titles associated with proper names, is usually well understood. Although there is hardly any departure from established custom, one occasionally sees curiosities. I have a guide-book in which the author makes a point of writing about "lord X." and "the duke of Y.," a discourteous practice equivalent to writing "mr." and "mrs."

Some writers have a fancy for putting well-worn clichés into capitals. By this means a writer lets his readers know that he is aware of using a cliché and is not just being tasteless or devoid of imagination. The device can be amusing if not overdone.

The four seasons—spring, summer, autumn, winter—do not require capitals.

Cardinal points of the compass should not be given capitals except in special circumstances or in abbreviations. The special circumstances are references to geographical regions, such as Northern Canada, the West of Scotland, the South Coast, the West Country, the North Pole, Southern China, Eastern Germany. It is also legitimate to write, "He comes from the North," or "Go West, young man!"

Ordinary references to cardinal points, however, should be given small letters, thus:

"The road forked six miles west of the town, and when I reached the junction I turned north-west. After a while I left the road and followed a path which led eastwards over a hill, a hill which seemed to be one of the foothills of a great mountain range that traversed the island from north to south."

In abbreviating directions you should insert any hyphens which may be necessary, as in "N.-N.-W." and "E.-S.-E." The omission of the hyphens, however, is quite common and is no great crime.

In the House of Commons the Member for Coketown is invariably given a capital M, while his political Party sometimes gets a capital P. The newspaper and periodical Press is usually given the capital to distinguish it from the printing-press from which it sprang. The Navy has a capital N, while *naval* can have a small n. Besides Her Majesty's Army there can be unofficial armies of people or ants or frogs.

In conclusion, I must again point out that capital letters must not be used carelessly or inconsistently. A passage of prose with capitals scattered before nouns for no reason at all is unattractive to the reader, certainly, but the main sufferer is the writer, who, perhaps wrongly, may be regarded as semi-literate.

SMALL CAPITALS

If a word is printed completely in *ordinary* capitals the effect is one of CLUMSINESS, isn't it? You feel that the writer is shouting at you. Sometimes, however, it is necessary to print whole words or groups of words in capitals, and to get over the difficulty and yet give a quiet tone to the page the printer may use SMALL CAPITALS.

Unfortunately, these characters are not on the keyboard of the typewriter, and if you are sending anything to be printed, and want the compositor to use small capitals, you should rule a double line under the words affected.

It is usual, for instance, to use small capitals for B.C. and A.D., which, I think you will agree, look much more tasteful in this form. It is worth remembering that the customary practice —though not the invariable practice—is to put "B.C." after the date and "A.D." before it, thus:

"Augustus Caesar (63 B.C. to A.D. 14) was the first Roman Emperor."

ITALICS

Italics are used in printing to emphasise something, to accentuate a word or group of words, to distinguish a word or group of words from the body of the text, and to show that a word or group of words is foreign. So much is generally known, and throughout this book there are dozens of examples of the use of italics.

These characters, however, like small capitals, do not form part of the keyboard of a normal typewriter, and if you want something to be printed in italics you underline it with a *single* line.

Printers seem to have a strange reluctance to print numerals in italics—I do not know why—and a Roman numeral in the middle of a line of italics looks odd, even unbalanced. It can be misleading, too, as in a title printed as "*Report on Proceedings, 1955.*" The year might be misinterpreted as the date of publication instead of the year of the proceedings, and the correct title is *Report on Proceedings, 1955.*

Some publishers use italics as an alternative to quotation marks for titles of books, periodicals, plays and films. In the case of a book or periodical, a reference to the title of anything contained *within* it should be in quotation marks, thus:

"In Mr. A.'s new book of essays, *The Changing Seasons*, the one which impresses me most is the fragile little *belle-lettre* entitled 'In the Park.' "

"Mr. B.'s article in yesterday's *Daily Trumpet*, 'Shall we have a new Party?', may lead to a barrage of questions when the House meets on Tuesday."

(Because of the question mark after the title of the article, the comma is given its logical place after the quotation mark instead of the conventional place before the quotation mark.)

Belle-lettre, as a French word, is printed in italics. It is quite satisfactory to use italics for foreign words and phrases, but a whole sentence in a foreign language can be tedious to read if printed in italics and should preferably be printed in Roman type.

CHAPTER IX

Common Mistakes-1

B<small>Y</small> "common mistakes" I do not mean the mistakes that are heard in the traditional maltreatment of English by the ignorant. I mean the mistakes made daily by people who claim to have enjoyed some education and who would feel deeply hurt if accused of not using their language correctly.

It might be expected that those whose living depends on the use of English—professional journalists and other writers, and public speakers—would be particular about their grammar. Unhappily this is not so, and practically every book, newspaper and magazine contains mistakes, while public speeches are seldom faultless. Is it surprising, then, that readers follow bad examples in the belief that anything in print, any public utterance, must be right?

Those people who are cocksure of their grammar hate being told of their mistakes, and of course anyone noticing the mistakes would be reluctant to point them out. There is a strong human instinct, from which good manners are derived, not to hurt or cause embarrassment, and there is also a strong instinct restraining the exhibition of any form of superiority in oneself.

I am afraid, therefore, that nothing can be done about the cocksure person, and it is better to suffer mistakes and keep the peace than to act as mentor and risk ill-feeling. The cocksure person might not read this book, but he might be brought down to earth from his fool's paradise if he realised his mistakes by reading faultless English in his books and his newspapers. It is easier to deal with the more tolerant person who is unsure of his English, for he will seldom be too vain to ask if a construction is correct.

I shall now work through the commoner mistakes, giving actual examples where possible. Many of these types of mistake have already been referred to in earlier chapters, and I hope you will excuse the frequent cross-references which will be necessary.

SUBJECT AND OBJECT

If you have read the earlier chapters, and if I have done my job properly, you should know by now the differences between the subject and the object of a sentence. Should you want to refresh yourself, you will find references in Chapter III (page 30), Chapter IV (page 49), Chapter V (pages 55 and 61) and Chapter VI (pages 72 and 74).

To summarise, I shall give examples of the confusion of subject and object with the necessary corrections:

Wrong	*Right*
"He took Mother and I for a ride in the car."	"He took Mother and me for a ride in the car."
"The manager met my friend and I at the station."	"The manager met my friend and me at the station."
"Between you and I . . ."	"Between you and me . . ."
"Come and sit beside we girls."	"Come and sit beside us girls."
"Me and the wife went to the pictures."	"My wife and I went to the pictures." (Note: Never refer to your wife as *the* wife.)
"It's me." (I admit that this is an accepted colloquialism.)	"It is I."
"Those are them."	"Those are they."
"Who shall I give it to?"	"Whom shall I give it to?"
"The person who I saw . . ."	"The person whom I saw . . ."
"Whom is the next speaker?"	"Who is the next speaker?"
"The man who the policeman arrested . . ."	"The man whom the policeman arrested . . ."

Finally, here is a gem from an estate agent's announcement:
"Mr. —— presents his compliments to he (or she) seeking, south of the Park, new, architect designed, freehold houses."

You will be aware that "he (or she)" should be "him (or her)." I should also point out that there should be a hyphen between "architect" and "designed," for the two words form a compound adjective.

"WHO" AND "WHOM"

Who is subjective, *whom* is objective.

"Who shall I give it to?" is wrong because the question is another form of "I shall give it to whom?" or "To whom shall I give it?" The subject is *I*, and a preposition—in this case *to*—is followed by the objective.

"Whom shall I take with me?" is right. "Who shall I take with me?" is wrong. *I* am taking *someone* with me, so that *I* is the subject, the *someone* is the object, and the someone in the question is the unknown *whom*.

Who, as the subject, is correct in such questions as the following:

"Who goes home?"
"Who is coming with me?"
"Who did it?"

When *who* is used as a simple relative pronoun (Chapter V, page 61) it is immaterial whether its governing noun or pronoun is the subject or the object, and both the following sentences are correct:

"The lady who dealt with the enquiry is away." ("The lady" is the subject.)

"I saw the man who did it." ("The man" is the object.)

We could also say, correctly: "The lady who is loved by all is away."

Yet *who* would be changed to *whom* in the following kinds of construction:

"The lady whom nothing could upset is away."
"The lady to whom you addressed your enquiry is away."

"The man whom the policeman arrested . . ." is right because it was the policeman who did the arresting. For *who* to be right, the man (subject) must himself have performed an action, or virtually performed it, as in "The man who was arrested . . ." Here, the man's action lay in being arrested.

The translators of the Psalms, though they sometimes erred in their English, made no mistake in the first verse of Psalm 27 (Prayer Book Version): "The Lord is my light, and my salvation; whom then shall I fear: the Lord is the strength of my life; of whom then shall I be afraid?"

"WHOSE"

Of *whose*, I do not think that I need say any more than I have said in Chapter V (page 62). All I shall repeat is that I do not like *whose* to be used for something impersonal, as in:

"At the outset of the meeting, whose agenda included a discussion on old-age pensions, the chairman gave a warning."

I prefer the following:

"At the outset of the meeting, of which the agenda"—or "the agenda of which"—"included a discussion on old-age pensions . . . ."

I like the use of *whose* to be confined to persons, as in the following two examples:

"The man whose car was stolen reported the facts to the police."

"Mrs. Jones, whose hundredth birthday fell yesterday, received presents from all her grand-children and great-grand-children."

"EVERY" AND "EACH"

I have dealt with *every*, *everyone* and *everything* fairly fully in Chapter V (page 68). The main thing to remember is that these are singular words, and it is a very common mistake to treat them as plurals.

Consider this example by a gossip-writer:

"I was most impressed by the reasonable prices and agreeable designs of everything on sale."

"Everything on sale" is singular, meaning *each* object, and each object had *its* own price and own design. The sentence should thus be:

"I was most impressed by the reasonable price and agreeable design of everything on sale."

"There are carpets in every room." This type of sentence is often heard. Each room *may* have more than one carpet, but the writer probably means that there is no room without a carpet. There are two correct ways of expressing the meaning:

"There is a carpet in every room."

"There are carpets in all the rooms."

Each is similarly maltreated, and the following are examples of common mistakes:

Wrong	*Right*
"The hotel issues free guide books to each guest."	"The hotel issues a free guide-book to each guest." *or* "The hotel issues free guide-books to all guests."
"I foresee neat rows of tiny houses, with smooth lawns in each garden and prams at each front door."	"I foresee neat rows of tiny houses, with a smooth lawn in each garden and a pram at each front door."

The following specimen is an extract from a bookseller's catalogue, following a list of novels by one author:

"Each are gripping examples of descriptive writing which many experienced writers in this genre might well envy."

A bookseller might be expected to know something of the English language, for indirectly his livelihood depends on it. However, this is only one bookseller, and it would be unfair to judge all booksellers by him. The sentence should, of course, be like this:

"Each is a gripping example of descriptive writing . . ."

Incidentally, the writer of the catalogue goes on to say, still of the same novelist: "Putting such matters aside he is a re-markable stylist." I hope that you know what is wrong with this sentence; if not, you will know later.

Each is singular, as I have explained, and is accompanied by the singular form of a verb. There is a pitfall, however, in this kind of sentence:

"Nigeria, Ghana, Sierra Leone and Gambia have each a part to play in the development of West Africa."

This is perfectly correct, but often you will find *has* instead of *have*. The plural verb *have* follows the enumeration of the different territories, but the singular *each* calls for *a part* (not *parts*). Alternatively, we could say:

"Nigeria, Ghana, Sierra Leone and Gambia all have parts to play in the development of West Africa."

"BETWEEN EACH"

It is indeed strange—in fact, it is incomprehensible—that one of the commonest mistakes is also one of the most obvious. Too often we read this kind of thing:

"Sow the plants in rows, with at least two feet between each row."

"The buttonholes should next be cut, with six inches between each."

"The Yorkshire Pennines are traversed by the Swale, the Ure and the Wharfe, between each of which is a range of hills forming a watershed."

It should be clear to anyone that the preposition *between* cannot exist with one singular word, and "between each" is nonsense. Correct versions of the foregoing sentences would be:

"Sow the plants in rows, with at least two feet between adjacent rows," *or* ". . . with at least two feet between each pair of rows," *or* "Sow the plants in rows, the rows being at least two feet apart."

"The buttonholes should next be cut, six inches apart."

"The Yorkshire Pennines are traversed by the Swale, the Ure and the Wharfe, each river being separated from the next by a range of hills forming a watershed."

I cannot resist the temptation to conclude this section by quoting a lapse by William Combe from his rich long poem, which is almost an epic, "Dr. Syntax's Tour in Search of the Picturesque" (1812):

> "Whoe'er has passed an idle hour,
> In following Syntax through his Tour,
> Must have perceiv'd he did not balk
> His fancy, when he wish'd to talk:
> Nay, more—that he was often prone
> To make long speeches when alone;
> And while he quaff'd th' inspiring ale,
> Between each glass to tell a tale: . . . ."

If Combe had substituted *between* by *after*, logic would have been satisfied and the line would still have scanned.

CONFUSION OF SINGULAR AND PLURAL

From consideration of *every* and *each* it is convenient to pass to the confusion of singular and plural within a sentence. Here are some examples of wrong and right:

Wrong	*Right*
"You cross all the rivers by a bridge."	"You cross all the rivers by bridges."
"There is a crisis in the life of all men."	"There are crises in the lives of all men."
"Scotland was made poorer by the death of Bruce and Wallace."	"Scotland was made poorer by the deaths of Bruce and Wallace."
"When leaving fields, please see that the gate is fastened."	"When leaving fields, please see that the gates are fastened."
"The towers are 20 ft. square at their base."	"The towers are 20 ft. square at their bases."

The conclusion is, then, that usually associated words in a sentence should agree *in number*—that is, singular with singular and plural with plural.

There are exceptions. Some words, for example, cannot be considered as plural, as the following sentences show:

"The dryness of the deserts is an adverse factor in their development" (not *drynesses*).

"The staff representation on the boards of the different companies is extremely active" (not *representations*).

"The atmosphere of West African countries is, in general, somewhat humid." (We should not use *atmospheres* here, although *atmosphere* has a plural in a quantitative scientific sense.)

I gave an example of the plural use of *death* in the sentence: "Scotland was made poorer by the deaths of Bruce and Wallace." Here, the death of each man is considered as a separate event. But if we refer to death in a general sense it can be singular, as in: "Death overtakes all men." "Deaths overtake all men" would sound queer.

There are doubtful cases – for example, "The foliage at the bottom of the mountains is different from that at the top."

If the mountains are altogether, it may be presumed that they have a common bottom, in which case "the bottom of the mountains" is right. But if the mountains are separated, each with its own bottom, then we should say "the bottoms of the mountains."

"EITHER" AND "NEITHER"

I explained in Chapter V (page 58) that while *either* is generally correctly used *neither* is often abused.

I once saw a glaring example of "neither are" in a newspaper's review of a book. I wrote to the editor, not pointing out the mistake but saying that readers expected a better standard of English. My letter was acknowledged courteously enough, but the editor apologised not for "neither are" but for the abnormal length of the sentence.

Here is an example:

"One can expect an immediate reaction from the Anti-Noise League, but neither the Clerk to the Magistrates nor the transport association's solicitor know of any regulations forbidding such cacophony."

As *Clerk* is singular, and *solicitor* is singular, *know* should be *knows*. *Know* would have been correct if both had been plural, as in:

"Neither the Clerks nor the solicitors know."

If one had been singular and the other plural there would have been a difficulty. Should we say "Neither the Clerks nor the solicitor know" or ". . . knows"?

There is no solution, and I should reconstruct the passage thus: "The Clerks do not know and the solicitor does not know."

Here is a very confused passage from a leading article:

"Neither the British nor the American Governments, who supply the major part of the country's national income, nor the French Government, which also contributes to her exchequer, were aware of the discussions until Sept. 25."

As I pointed out on page 59, "neither . . . nor" should not be used if there are more than two items. Yet here we have three items—the British, American and French Governments. That is one mistake. Another mistake is to say "neither . . . were."

A third mistake is to say "Neither the British nor the American Governments" (instead of "Government"). A fourth is to use *who* for the British and American Governments and *which* for the French Government; there should be consistency, expecially when there is a reference to *her* exchequer.

The sentence is so hopelessly confused that it is beyond simple correction. It is a case that is crying out for drastic rewriting, and, not forgetting to change "major part" for "most," I should do it thus:

"The British and the American Governments, who supply most of the country's national income, and the French Government, who also contributes to her exchequer, were not aware of the discussions until Sept. 25."

THE USE OF ADJECTIVES AS ADVERBS

"Do it quick" is wrong. *Quick* is an adjective, and the verb *do* demands an adverb. The correct version is "Do it quickly." Similarly, "Drive slow" should be "Drive slowly."

While it is colloquial to say "Walk quicker" and "Drive slower," the correct forms are "Walk more quickly" and Drive more slowly."

Fast, on the other hand, is both adjective and adverb. Another curious inconsistency concerns *wrong* and *right*. We say "He did his sums wrongly" but "He did his sums right." Yet if both terms are used together we say "Rightly or wrongly."

We speak of a tradition or a convention as "dying hard," meaning that the tradition or convention finds it hard to die. It would seem strange to say "die hardly," as *hardly* means *scarcely* or *nearly*.

Well is the adverb corresponding with the adjective *good*. Thus, we say "She is a good singer" or "She sings well." Some people, unfortunately, think it sounds polite to use *well* when they mean *good*, and frequently we hear: "It looks well on her, doesn't it?"

This construction is wrong. The word *well* is not associated with the verb *looks* but with the pronoun *it*, so that the adjective *good* should be used. The correct form of the sentence, in the sense meant by the polite speaker, is: "It looks good on her, doesn't it?" The same speaker would have no doubts at all about saying, correctly, "It looks splendid" or "It looks horrible" or "It looks old-fashioned."

Literally, "It looks well" means that *it* performs the *act of looking* well. *Well* is also an adjective meaning healthy, and although "He looks well" usually means that he looks healthy, it could also mean that he is a good performer in the act of looking.

REDUNDANT CONDITIONALS

The redundant conditional is the name I have given to the laboured form of construction described on page 47, Chapter IV. An example is the following:

"I should have thought that it would have been better the other way."

This is logically wrong as well as grammatically wrong. You cannot have two conditionals with one compound clause. There are two correct alternatives:

"I should have thought that it was better the other way."

"I think it would have been better the other way."

A somewhat similar form of redundancy is exhibited in the use of past participles, but that will come later.

UNFORMED SENTENCES

I gave some examples of unformed "sentences" (though they are not sentences) under the headings "Definition of a Sentence" and "Slovenly Examples" in Chapter VI.

Besides these examples, there are those groups of words, spoken, written or printed each day, that start with *which*, like these:

"The Government of ——, though lethargic in the implementation of its foreign policy, is at least stable. Which cannot be said for the Government of the neighbouring territory."

"My uncle gave me a pound and told me to go and enjoy myself. Which I thereupon proceeded to do with alacrity."

"Defending counsel described his client as industrious and honest, a man of integrity. Which, of course, he isn't."

There are two main errors of thought and grammar in slipshod passages like these. One error lies in the fact that in each case the "sentence" starting with *which* is not a sentence at all, but is a secondary clause dependent on the previous sentence. There should, therefore, be neither a full-stop after the previous sentence nor a capital *W*.

The second error is in the assumption that the relative pronoun *which* can be used to relate a clause to something other than a noun or pronoun. This "something," in the first example, is the statement that the Government is stable. In the second example it is the uncle's command "to go and enjoy myself."

In the third example the "something" is defending counsel's opinion of his client's virtues.

Which, as a relative pronoun, can only be used directly with a noun or a pronoun. The three examples above, then, cannot be corrected simply by the changing of each full-stop to a comma and of each capital *W* to a small *w*. The passages must be reconstructed, and my suggestions would be the following:

"The Government of ——, though lethargic in the implementation of its foreign policy, is at least stable, and that is something that cannot be said for the Government of the neighbouring territory."

"My uncle gave me a pound and told me to go and enjoy myself. I thereupon proceeded to do so with alacrity."

"Defending counsel described his client as industrious and honest, a man of integrity. He is, in fact, nothing of the sort."

The examples given, of unformed sentences starting with *Which,* are similar to the example given on page 72: "To whom the book may be recommended."

There are other kinds of unformed sentences, and here are some curious examples from Fleet Street:

"The setting was an interview between Mr. X, the M.P. who has recently been conducting a stormy correspondence in *The Times* about workmen on a building site spending too much time making tea." (How could Mr. X have an interview between himself?)

"They prove that . . . . one can do it beautifully. Or at any rate, with attractive accessories. Also practically." (There is far too much of this kind of journalism.)

"Mr. Nutting, now in New York, is a snorkel fan. So is Mr. Selwyn Lloyd, which led to his undoing." (This could be corrected by the insertion of "a fact" between the comma and "which.")

"INCLUDE" AND "INCLUDING"

Though it is debatable whether the verb "to include" was originally meant to embrace a whole or only a part, present usage generally carries the second implication.

"The C.B.I. includes many thousands of smaller firms which are not directly represented on its councils."

Obviously the thousands of smaller firms do not make up the whole of the C.B.I. There is nothing wrong, however, in giving the verb "to include" a much more comprehensive meaning, and we are equally justified in saying:

"The C.B.I. includes such industrial giants as The Rover Group, I.C.I., Courtaulds, as well as many thousands of smaller firms which are not directly represented on its councils."

It is possible to make a mistake with *include*, as in this short extract from a cookery guide:

"Some of the Chinese foods you can buy include: . . ."

Some and *include* are similar in implication, and the cookery writer should have written either of the following:

"Some of the Chinese foods you can buy are: . . ."

"The Chinese foods you can buy include: . . ."

The modern understanding that the verb "to include" embraces only a part, and not the whole, is obvious from the very common use of the present participle *including*.

"The members, including children, number over a thousand." Not all the members are children. Incidentally, it is important to note that the present participle *including* must be related to a noun or a pronoun, the related word in this case being the noun *members*.

"CHART" AND "CHARTER"

A *chart* is a map or a plan. Thus, the verb "to chart" means to map, or to plot a survey. An uncharted reef is a reef not shown on a chart, or nautical map.

Yet here is an extract from a newspaper:

"A party of holidaymakers, rescued in motor launches when their boat struck an unchartered reef, were landed at Southampton."

The word should be *uncharted*. The verb "to charter" means to hire, and the noun "charter" is a Royal documentary instrument.

Some people explode when they see *Magna Charta*, and point out that it should be *Magna Carta*, the Great Charter. Their fury is wasted, however, for in Latin the two words are synonymous. *Magna Carta* happens to be the commoner form

"DUE TO"

"The scheme was not approved due to the absence of water in the vicinity."

"Rule Seven is invalid, due to its inacceptance by a minority of members."

"Due to the inclement weather, the annual outing has been postponed till next week."

All these are wrong.

Due to can only be used to link two nouns. Only "something" can be *due to* something else, and the following are quite right:

"His sleeplessness was due to late meals."

"General resentment, due mainly to the high-handed actions of the committee, was felt by all the members."

"Can the incidence of juvenile delinquency be due to the lack of parental interest?"

Consider the wrong sentences again. Could the first be written thus? "Disapproval of the scheme was due to the absence of water."

This is correct structurally, but not quite correct logically. The listener or reader is first *being told* of something, namely, that the scheme was not approved, the reason for the disapproval following.

To say or write the sentence in the manner just given would imply that the listener already knows of the disapproval and is now being told the reason. If we wanted to use *due to* here, one way would be this:

"The scheme was not approved, the disapproval being due to the absence of water in the vicinity."

The other two examples could be rewritten thus:

"Rule Seven is invalid, the invalidity being due to its inacceptance by a minority of members."

"The annual outing has been postponed till next week, the postponement being due to the inclement weather."

If, however, we want to stick to the same kind of construction but avoid the misuse of *due to*, the following are the simplest ways:

"The scheme was not approved, because of the absence of water in the vicinity." (The comma is essential. If it is omitted the sentence can imply that the scheme *was* approved but for other reasons than the absence of water.)

"Rule Seven, being inacceptable by a minority of members, is invalid."

"Because of the inclement weather, the annual outing has been postponed till next week."

Dr. J. Bronowski, reviewing a book by Dr. Fred Hoyle, rightly castigated the author for having written: "Stars can collapse catastrophically due to this cause."

Owing to can sometimes be used instead of *because of*, but I do not care for *on account of*, which is clumsy. *On account of*, moreover, lends itself to such horrible Americanisms as the following: "I went home from the office on account of I was feeling ill." Fortunately this kind of monstrosity has not yet invaded popular English speech.

"REASON"

From consideration of *due to* we pass conveniently to some observations on the associated constructions containing *reason*.

"The reason I am going home" is equivalent to "Why I am going home." It is just another way of saying it.

"The reason why I am going home," therefore, contains a redundancy, or duplication of meaning.

Why should not be used after the noun *reason* unless it is necessary as a convenient link for the sake of smoothness. "There is no reason I should go home" sounds awkward, and it is more usual to say "There is no reason why I should go home." The use of *why* could be avoided if the speaker said "There is no reason for my going home."

Another common error of duplication to avoid with the noun *reason* is its use in such constructions as "The reason is because . . ." and "The reason is due to . . ." The reason for something obviously cannot be because of or due to anything.

A mother may write to a schoolteacher: "The reason for my boy's absence was due to an attack of measles." This kind of mistake is not uncommon, and either of the following two correct forms could be used:

"The reason for my boy's absence was an attack of measles."

"My boy's absence was due to an attack of measles."

The verb *to reason why* can be quite correct. The verb implies a particular reasoning, a reasoning of some problem, while *to reason* simply implies reasoning in general. *To reason why* implies that the object of the reasoning is to find out the cause of something, so that when Tennyson wrote "Theirs not to reason why" he was probably justified. (Tennyson, wrongly, wrote "their's," and many editors omit the apostrophe.)

"CIRCUMSTANCES"

Circumstances are the events *around* something. Therefore to say "under the circumstances" is wrong. The correct use is "in the circumstances."

OMISSION OF ARTICLES

In Chapter II, page 24, I criticised some sections of the Press for having developed an unpleasant custom of omitting the definite article *the* and the indefinite articles *a* and *an*. Here is an example of this kind of slovenly writing:

"Best part for holiday this year is South Coast. If weather is good there are several resorts to give you variety of entertainment. At Seacliff try pierrots. At Sunbeach don't miss hanging gardens. Eastwater offers marble bathing pool. Westwater boasts biggest aerial ride in Europe. Special attraction at Mudflat Kursaal this year is thriller *Hamlet* on ice with all-star skating and bathing cast. All these exciting places are honoured by Holiday Guide recommends."

I do not want to rewrite this dreadful piece of vulgarity and insert the articles where necessary. You can do it yourself. I must point out two things, however. "Bathing-pool" needs a hyphen; otherwise it means a pool which is bathing. Then, to make the verb "recommend" into a noun is atrocious, for there happens to be a noun, "recommendation." You will hear, similarly, an invitation called an "invite," but these practices are indefensible.

"THOSE KIND"

I cannot understand the crime of saying "those kind," which seems to be on the increase among writers and public speakers. As I begged in Chapter V, you must never say "those kind" of anything. You can say "those kinds," "these kinds," "this kind" or "that kind." But to say "those kind" is to apply a plural adjective to a singular noun.

THE MISUSE OF "AN"

The indefinite article *an* is used before a word starting with a *vowel sound*—not necessarily with a vowel.

Unique, for example, starts with a vowel but a vowel having the effect of a *y*. It is foolish to say or write "an unique," a mistake which is incomprehensible, for nobody would ever think of saying "an unicorn."

It is equally wrong and incomprehensible to say or write "an hotel," yet you come across this fault every day. It is right to say "an hour" and "an honour," when the *h* is silent, but please say "*a* hotel."

"AT ABOUT"

"I shall expect you about five o'clock."
"I shall expect you at about five o'clock."
Which of these is correct?

Strictly, *at* applies to a definite time; *about* applies to an approximate time. Therefore, *at about* is a confusion of two unlikes, and should be avoided. I commend the logically-minded people who say: "I shall expect you at or about five o'clock."

"FACE UP TO"

The 1939-1945 war produced many additions to our language, most of them unwelcome. One horrible addition was the compound verb "to face up" to anything.

Today nearly everyone seems to use it; even writers and the B.B.C. are not guiltless. What is wrong with the verb "to face"? Why should "up to" be added?

"I could not face up to the problem."
Is this an improvement on "I could not face the problem"?

Of course it isn't. Additions to a language can only be justified if they are necessities or improvements, and "face up to" is in neither category.

"STAND FOR"

"Stand for," instead of simply "stand," meaning "tolerate," is another modern expression in the same hateful class as "face up to." The addition of the preposition "for" is quite needless.

"I'm not standing for it."

Is this any more effective than "I'm not standing it"?

"Stand for," of course, has legitimate meanings, too, as in: "He is standing for Parliament."

"B.B.C. stands for British Broadcasting Corporation."

" 'I stand for righteousness and justice,' said the street-corner orator."

OTHER VERBS WITH PREPOSITIONS

The harshness of "face up to" and "stand for" is emphasised by their newness. There are many similar compound verbs which are equally disreputable but which have acquired a spurious respectability simply through the softening effect of age. Examples of such verbs are the following: "start up," "stop up," "speed up," "slow down," "heat up," "try out," "add up," "seek out."

I cannot defend the use of the prepositions in these examples, On the other hand, "give up" and "cough up" are different from "give" and "cough."

There is a peculiar Americanism—"visit with" for "visit," as in "We visited with some friends in New York." The unattractive habit of saying "consult with" (for "consult") has even spread to the United Kingdom, and there is the incomprehensible construction, "meet up with," instead of the simple "meet."

"PERPENDICULAR" AND "VERTICAL"

Perpendicular is often misused for *vertical*.

Any line at right-angles to any other line, or any plane at right-angles to any other plane, is perpendicular to it, though it need not be vertical.

A vertical line is at right-angles to the horizontal, the horizontal being a direction parallel with the earth's surface.

It is most unfortunate that the mistake of using *perpendicular* for *vertical* has been perpetuated by the so-called Perpendicular style of architecture.

"PARALLEL WITH"

Two lines can be *parallel with* one another (or each other), not *parallel to* one another. The preposition *to* signifies approach, and the moment the lines start approaching each other they cease to be parallel.

"COMPARE"

There is some confusion about "compare with" and "compare to." Some pedagogues insist on *with* in comparison of unlike subjects and *to* in comparison of likes. I avoid dogmatism on this matter, but in my opinion the opposite view is more logical—*with* being more suitable for comparison of likes, or subjects which are supposedly similar, and *to* for comparison of subjects in which the likeness is somewhat remote. My personal constructions would be as in the following:

"Can Marlowe be compared *with* Shakespeare?"

"The state of agriculture in Mangrovia, compared *with* that in Gozoland, is, according to the White Paper, a matter for debate."

"The English master, praising Jim Brown's essays, jocularly compared the boy *to* Bacon."

"As the rabbit dodged into the bracken I compared the little animal *to* a cunning lion in the African jungle."

Sometimes you may be uncertain whether the compared subjects are like or unlike each other, and in such cases *with* is safer. *With* is invariably used in such constructions as: "For durability of footwear, nothing can compare *with* leather."

"USED TO"

"He used to live in London" means "He formerly lived in London" or "He once lived in London."

That is understood. But neither the past tense nor the negative is generally understood, and we hear constructions like these:

"He didn't use to live in London."

"Did he use to live in London?"

"Used to" is itself a peculiar idiom, but there is no point in making its variations even more peculiar. The correct versions of the two examples are:

"He used not to live in London."

"Used he to live in London?"

"PROMISE"

To *promise* means to engage oneself to perform a future act, to give a definite undertaking for the future.

So much is generally understood. But in recent years the verb has acquired a further meaning and is now used, quite wrongly, to indicate that one is telling the truth at the moment. You may hear this kind of sentence:

"As I was coming home I saw a pink monkey, I promise you."

This use of *promise* is unjustified. To be correct the speaker could have said: "As I was coming home I saw a pink monkey, I swear."

CHAPTER X

Common Mistakes - 2

‒‒‒‒‒‒‒‒‒‒‒‒‒‒‒‒‒‒‒‒‒‒‒‒‒‒‒‒‒‒

IN our journey through the jungle of common mistakes we have come about half-way. I am not yet tired—nor, I hope, are you—and when we emerge at the end of this chapter I trust that I shall have enabled you to see the clear sky with new vision. Let us proceed.

"OUGHT TO"

Nearly every day I hear someone say "He ought to, didn't he?"

This is something I cannot understand, as it is used by people who consider themselves educated. The correct construction, of course, is "He ought to, oughtn't he?" or ". . . ought he not?"

The mistake—if it can be called a mistake instead of gross insensitivity—is particularly prevalent in parts of the Midlands of England.

"LAY" AND "LIE"

In the use of *lay* and *lie*, and their derivatives, I cannot do better than refer you to an earlier chapter (Chapter IV, page 50).

"ATTAIN"

To attain means to reach, or to arrive, in the sense of reaching a height or arriving at a goal. Often it is used figuratively, as in "He attained the Presidency" or "He attained his dearest ambition."

149

Sometimes, however, *to* is added unnecessarily. "You can attain to something higher" is wrong. It is equivalent to saying "You can reach to something higher." Mountaineers do not try to attain to the summit; they try to attain the summit.

"DIFFERENT FROM"

In spite of various feeble attempts at defence, "different to" is wrong simply because it is illogical. Nobody would dream of saying "similar from."

It is most unfortunate that "different to" has penetrated such respectable quarters as Parliament, literature and the Press, for in matters of English many people accept the guidance of these mentors. They are even guilty of using an offensive import from America, "different than," which is meaningless rather than illogical.

"TRY AND"

Many people say "try and" when they mean "try to." Mistakes apart, however, there is a subtle difference between the two expressions.

Logically, if you try *and* do something you *try* first, making a general attempt in the right direction and finding out how to do it. Having found out the best way of doing it, you *do* it. Thus there are two actions involved, the trying and the doing, and in this sense "try and" can be quite right.

"Try to," on the other hand, implies the single combined action of trying and doing. Usually the correct expression is "try to," and when people say "try and" they seldom have the logical meaning in mind.

"TIMES GREATER THAN"

"Production this year is six times greater than production last year."

What exactly does this mean?

If production is *once* greater, it is as much again, or twice as much as before. If it is *twice* greater, it is three times as much as before.

Therefore, if production (or anything else) is x times greater, it is $(x + 1)$ times as great as before.

This is simple, isn't it? Nothing could be more logical. And yet, the person who wrote that sentence—"Production this year is six times greater than production last year"—actually meant that production is *six times as great*.

If the sentence is interpreted literally, it means that production this year is seven times production last year.

This is a very common type of mistake, especially in journalism, and you must be careful about it.

"EXTENDED TOUR"

When a bus company advertises "Extended tours to the Highlands" it is writing nonsense.

"Extended" means "made longer" or "lengthened." Thus an *extended* tour is a tour which has been increased above its original length. In other words, the company originally meant it to last for a certain time but has now decided to extend or prolong it.

Nothing could be further, of course, from the company's mind, or minds. The intended meaning is that the tour to the Highlands (or the South-West, or the Lake District, or the Continent) is quite long as tours go, and the word that should be used is *extensive*.

Unfortunately, the companies having started to talk about "extended tours," some of the public are accepting it as English. Do not encourage your friends in this lapse.

"BUT, HOWEVER"

Occasionally, one comes across this kind of construction:

"A blizzard had raged all morning, our limbs were numbed and our bodies exhausted. We expected to find a roaring fire of comfort in the cabin. But when we arrived, however, and opened the door, all we found was a cold heap of ashes in the hearth."

But and *however* are similar in effect, and should not be used together. The second sentence of this passage can be expressed in either of the following two ways:

"But when we arrived, and opened the door, all we found was a cold heap of ashes . . . ."

"When we arrived, however, and opened the door, all we found was a cold heap of ashes . . . ."

"LOAN" AND "LEND"

Loan is a noun. *Lend* is a verb. It is a foolish and common mistake, however, to use *loan* as a verb, as in "I loaned him a fiver" instead of "I lent him a fiver." When something is *on loan* it is *lent*.

"LEARN" FOR "TEACH"

I have a particular reason for talking about the misuse of *learn* for *teach*. To say "I'll learn you" is a sign of illiteracy, and I certainly do not expect my readers to be illiterate.

My reason for mentioning it is found in the *Book of Common Prayer*, and is a warning that the text of the Prayer Book is not to be accepted in its entirety as good English, even as good mediaeval English.

In the Prayer Book, verse 4 of Psalm 25 is thus:

"Lead me forth in thy truth, and learn me: for thou art the God of my salvation; . . . ."

In the Bible, the fifth verse of Psalm 25 is thus:

"Lead me in thy truth, and teach me: for thou art the God of my salvation; . . . ."

(The first two verses of the Biblical version are condensed into the first verse of the Prayer Book version; hence the Bible's verse 5 is the Prayer Book's verse 4.)

THE MISUSE OF "THAT"

It grieves me exceedingly that a horrible practice has crept into English and is used shamelessly by many people who should know better. I refer to the use of *that* with an adjective, as in the following dreadful sentences:

"I had no idea the house was that small."

"As a pianist he isn't really that good."

"If the weather is that bad you had better stay at home."

In spite of common acceptance, this use of *that* is wrong and is to be avoided. The correct forms of the above sentences are:

"I had no idea that the house was as small as that." (The omission of "that" after "idea" is a permissible colloquialism.)

"As a pianist he isn't really as good as that."

"If the weather is as bad as that you had better stay at home."
That is often used instead of a simple *so*:

"I was that happy I could have cried."

"I went to the pictures three times that week, the film was that exciting."

"That happy" and "that exciting" should be "so happy" and "so exciting."

The common expressions "that much" and "that many" should be "as much as that" and "as many as that."

"RIGHT HERE"

"Right here," "right there" and "right now" are Americanisms which I can hardly call mistakes. I have heard them on Children's Television, but people with any respect for English avoid them. That is all I shall say.

"CHRISTMAS"

The only excuse for writing "Xmas" for "Christmas" is that *X* was the Greek symbol for Jesus Christ. Some people, aware of this, do it deliberately, but most writers of "Xmas" are merely lazy.

"MOOT POINT"

A moot point, something to be debated, discussed and pondered over, derives its name from the Anglo-Saxon town assembly, or court of justice, which was a *moot* or *mote*, while the meeting-place was the moot hall.

Unfortunately many people confuse the word *moot* with *mute* (silent), and wrongly talk about a "mute point" instead of a "moot point."

"ALL RIGHT"

Already, almost, almighty and *altogether* are right, but *alright* is wrong. I confess that there seems to be no fair reason for this, yet those who insist on writing "alright" are branded as semi-ignorant.

If you want your written English to be acceptable, therefore, you must write "all right."

"AVERSE FROM"

You are not *averse to*, or show an *aversion to*, anything. The suffix *to* signifies approach, when the opposite is intended. You can only be *averse from*, òr show an *aversion from*, something.

CONFUSED WORDS

Certain pairs of similar words are often confused and wrongly used, one word of a pair being used in place of the other. The following cases are the most common, and will be dealt with in turn:

deprecate and *depreciate;*   *licence* and *license;*
loathe and *loath (loth)*;   *prescribe* and *proscribe;*
for go and *fore go;*   *dependent* and *dependant;*
forbear and *forebear;*   *effect* and *affect;*
barmy and *balmy;*   *adopt* and *adapt.*

"DEPRECATE" AND "DEPRECIATE"

Deprecate, meaning "pray against," is the opposite to "pray for."

Depreciate, meaning (in one sense) "disparage," is the opposite to "praise."

These two verbs, and their derivatives, are often confused. The confusion is not due solely to the similar appearance of the words, but also to the fact that sometimes they can be very similar in meaning. Consider this sentence:

"The City Architect deprecated the tendency of the Works Department to allow famous buildings to get into bad states of neglect."

The City Architect could have been either praying against the tendency—that is, wishing that the tendency was absent—or disparaging it. Int his case, therefore, either *deprecated* or *depreciated* could be used with similar effect.

If, instead of praying for our enemies (as morally we should), we pray against them, we *deprecate* them, just as we deprecate all the things we should not pray for—war, disease, famine, suffering. Yet often *deprecate* (or one of its derivatives) is used instead of *depreciate* (or one of its derivatives), as in the following two examples:

"Self-deprecation is a virtue of the humble-minded."

"The chairman, publicly deprecating the committee's rash action, rose and left the room."

Ask yourself the meaning of each sentence.

Does the first mean that the humble-minded pray against themselves or disparage themselves? They are not likely to pray against themselves, and the obvious meaning is that they disparage themselves. The correct expression, then, is "self-depreciation."

In the second sentence, is the chairman praying against the committee's action or disparaging it? I think he is certainly disparaging it, so that the word should be "depreciating."

I said that *depreciate*, in one sense, meant disparage. In another sense, of course, it means decline in value, but then it is used intransitively, as in: "The value of the machine depreciates by 20 per cent. each year, and will thus be written off in five years."

"LOATHE" AND "LOATH"

Loathe is the verb, meaning detest or hate. *Loath* is an adjective, meaning unwilling or reluctant.

Loth is simply another form of "loath," and is used mainly in the strange idiom, "nothing loth," which means "eager" or "willing." "When asked if he would like a half-holiday, Jim, nothing loth, accepted the master's offer."

It is quite common to find *loathe* and *loath* confused:

"I loath travelling by train" (instead of *loathe*).

"Though loathe to leave home, he went abroad to seek his fortune" (instead of *loath*).

Loathing is a present participle often used as a noun, as in: "He viewed the scene with loathing."

"FORGO" AND "FOREGO"

To *forgo* means to give up, and to *forego* means to precede, to go before.

Yet very frequently *forego* is wrongly used instead of *forgo*, as in:

"Will you promise to forego your half-holiday if I grant you this favour?" Here, *forego* should be *forgo*.

Perhaps the reason for the error is the fact that *forego* in its correct sense has fallen into disuse. There are so many other *fore-* words that people may forget that *for-* words exist as well. *Forget* is one of them.

"FORBEAR" AND "FOREBEAR"

The remarks in the last paragraph apply to *forbear* and *forebear*. To *forbear* means to suffer in patience, to hold oneself in check. A *forebear* is an ancestor.

"BARMY" AND "BALMY"

These two words are often confused. *Barmy* (from *barm*, which is another name for yeast) literally means "frothy," but more often the meaning is extended to "slightly mad." *Balmy* (from *balm*, a fragrant juice, ointment or oil) means "soft, soothing, fragrant, mild." The correct usages are shown in the following sentences:

"You must be barmy to believe everything he tells you."

"Isn't it a wonderfully balmy evening!"

(The second sentence, although couched as a question, is meant as an exclamation, and therefore receives the exclamation mark rather than the question mark.)

"LICENCE" AND "LICENSE"

Licence is the noun. *License* is the verb.

A *licensed* house can have a seven-day *licence*. The landlord is the *licensee*.

"PRESCRIBE" AND "PROSCRIBE"

To *prescribe* means to lay down with authority, to direct something for use as a remedy, to assert a prescriptive title. Its usual application is in connection with medicine.

To *proscribe* is to publish the name of something as doomed or condemned, to outlaw, to banish, to forbid, to denounce as dangerous. Thus, an organisation or a publication can be proscribed by a government, an authority or anyone else who considers it is dangerous, subversive or seditious. By modern

general usage, however, there is no implication that the proscribed organisation or publication must cease to exist.

"DEPENDENT" AND "DEPENDANT"

Dependent and *independent* are adjectives.

"He is dependent on me."

"The *Daily Reflection* is independent of party, creed and
sectional interests."

"Prisoner was described as of independent means."

Dependant is a noun, being someone or something dependent
on someone or something else.

"As a married man and a father I have several dependants
who look to me for support."

These words are often confused, the greater tendency being
to use *dependant* for *dependent*.

"EFFECT" AND "AFFECT"

Effect and *affect* give rise to much muddled thinking.

Effect can be both a noun and a verb. Here it is as a noun:

"The effect of the speech was to electrify the audience."

"Certain drugs have a soporific effect."

"Independence may have the effect of arrogance."

Here is *effect* as a verb, meaning "bring about":

"The judge said he hoped the arrangement would effect a
reconciliation between the parties."

"After much heated discussion the disputants appealed to
the chairman, who recommended that a compromise be effected
without delay."

"Effecting the right degree of temperature in the furnace is a
matter of great skill."

It should be noted that the verb *effect* is always transitive.

Affect is also a verb, and *only* a verb. When used transitively
it means "have an effect on."

"The only matter now affecting the issue is the legal right of
the lessee to enter the land."

"Onions do not affect my eyes as they do other people's."

"She was visibly affected by the sad proceedings."

Affect can also be used intransitively to mean "pretend,"
but in this sense it is always followed by "to," as in:

"He affects to be a wealthy man."

"She affects to be a woman of no importance."

This meaning of *affect* gives the noun *affectation* (pretence).

"ADOPT" AND "ADAPT"

"We shall adopt, as our motto, 'Nil desperandum'."

"At last they decided to adopt a child."

"The play is adapted from the German."

"We could adapt the curtains to fit the windows of the new house."

Hardly anyone finds any trouble in the use of the verbs *adopt* and *adapt*. I have seen evidence of confusion, however, in the derived nouns *adoption* and *adaptation*. It is not uncommon to see or hear *adaption*, the only fault in the use of which seems to be a lack of observation.

Incidentally, it is absurd to speak of an "adopted parent." The adjective here should be *adoptive*.

"SCAN"

Too many people give *scan* the directly opposite meaning to its real meaning. To scan anything does not mean to glance at it hurriedly. It means to scrutinise it thoroughly, to digest it properly, to get the full flavour or interpretation of it.

Grammar is like law in that ignorance is no excuse, and there is no excuse for misuse of *scan*.

There is the associated meaning of *scan*, of course, as applied to verse. To scan a line of verse is to count its metrical feet, a foot being a group of syllables on one beat.

Thus, Gray's line, "The lowing herd winds slowly o'er the lea," is scanned thus:

"The low/ing herd/ winds slow/ly o'er/ the lea."

I hope you will forgive this short digression, but if you are sufficiently interested in English to read this book you should be interested in verse. As there are five feet in this line (divided by oblique strokes), the line is called a *pentameter*. Each foot is of two syllables, one short and one long, and this kind of foot is called an *iambus*. The line is thus an *iambic pentameter*, and although a simple form of poetic construction it has immense capabilities. For a study of iambic pentameters you cannot do better than read Shakespeare.

REDUNDANT PAST PARTICIPLES

Redundant past participles are rather similar to redundant conditionals (page 47).

"He would have had to have waited" contains two past participles (*had* and *waited*) when only one is necessary. The meaning of this sentence should be expressed thus:

"He would have had to wait."

UNATTACHED PARTICIPLES

Now we come to a class of error which is probably the most common of all—so common, in fact, that I have left it almost to the last.

Always remember this: *a present participle must be logically attached to a noun or a pronoun.*

Participles in general are dealt with in Chapter IV (page 40). An example of an unattached present participle is given in Chapter VI (page 71) in the sentence:

"Referring to your letter of the 16th November, the horse was sold last Monday."

If this is strictly interpreted, the present participle *referring* is attached to *the horse*. But the writer does not really mean that the horse was referring to the letter of the 16th November. He means that he himself is referring to the letter. There are several ways in which the sentence could be made sensible, and here is one:

"Referring to your letter of the 16th November, I have to state that the horse was sold last Monday."

"I have to state" is commercial English, but at least the sentence is now grammatical, with the participle *referring* attached to the pronoun *I*.

This silly kind of mistake is extremely prevalent in commercial correspondence. Think, too, of the common misuse of *providing*, as in:

"Providing the goods are despatched by the end of December we shall pay in full by the end of January."

Literally, this means that *we* are doing the *providing*, and this, of course, is nonsense. The word here should be the past participle *provided*.

Here is a newspaper paragraph:

"Providing the weather is suitable, the Queen and the Duke of Edinburgh intend to take next month a week's cruise in the Mediterranean."

The Queen and the Duke have enough to think about without providing that the weather is suitable, and here, too, the word should be *provided*.

"ASSUMING"

We are still in our study of unattached participles, and our next target is *assuming*. This kind of construction is common:

"Assuming it does not rain, the match will take place as arranged."

This means that the match will do the assuming, when actually the assuming is done by the organisers of the match. If the writer wants to use the word *assuming* he should write the sentence this way:

"Assuming it does not rain, the organisers will see tnat the match takes place as arranged."

I should prefer, however, to call in the aid of the past participle *assumed*, like this:

"It being assumed that it does not rain"—or "will not rain"—"the match will take place as arranged."

Here is another example:

"The stage is set for a dramatic dénouement of the crisis in the Middle East by the deadline of Monday next, assuming—which is far from certain—that a great gamble by the President of the United States comes off."

The present participle *assuming* is not attached to anything. And it is difficult to see what the relative pronoun *which* is related to. The writer should have expressed this passage something like this:

"The stage is set for a dramatic dénouement of the crisis in the Middle East by the deadline of Monday next, it being assumed that a great gamble by the President of the United States comes off. It is, however, far from certain if it will come off."

"JUDGING"

Many professional journalists are fond of the present participle *judging* and often use it wrongly. Here is one example:

"Judging by accounts in the British Press, the opening night of *The Phantom of the Opera* in New York seems to have been successful."

This means that the opening night did the judging. The use of *judged* would have saved the situation.

Here is another passage where *judged* should have been used instead of *judging*:

"Judging by the department stores' sales, this looks like being France's most prosperous Christmas ever."

MISCELLANEOUS EXAMPLES OF UNATTACHED PARTICIPLES

Prevalent errors are in the use of "broadly speaking," "strictly speaking," "generally speaking," and all the other kinds of speaking.

"Broadly speaking, the fortunes of the catering trade depend on the weather."

Can it be the fortunes of the catering trade which speak broadly? This sentence would have made sense if "speaking" had been omitted.

Then there is the other old friend which appears in all the picture papers, in respectable newspapers and on picture postcards: "Beach at Seahampton, looking east."

The reader or viewer is meant to assume that *he* is looking east. But the literal meaning is that the beach itself is looking east—the direct opposite to the meaning intended.

The following is from a literary article by a *former editor*: "Looking back, then, two editors are outstanding . . . ." The passage should be reconstructed: "If we look back," or "If one looks back, then, two editors are outstanding . . . ."

How do you like the following confused passage?

"Having made this quite clear it can be stated, for what it is worth, that since nationalization Bolivian tin has been sold at prices averaging a dollar and less and has cost from a dollar and a half to two dollars to produce, converting costs at the official exchange rate."

As it stands, the present participle *having* is attached to the pronoun *it*. Nobody knows what *it* is, but whatever it is it is not the thing that has made "this quite clear." It is hard to find anything at all to which *converting* might be attached.

Here is a grammatical reconstruction:

"This having been made quite clear, it can be stated, for what it is worth, that although, since nationalisation, Bolivian tin has cost one and a half to two dollars to produce, it has been sold at prices (costs being converted at the official exchange rate) averaging a dollar and less."

This is a grammatical reconstruction, but it still is not very good prose. I have had to insert several commas to divide the long sentence into logical groups, but the effect is jerky. A much better way of writing the passage would be thus:

"The foregoing has been made quite clear. It may be of interest that although, since nationalisation, Bolivian tin has cost one and a half to two dollars to produce, its average selling price at the official exchange rate has averaged a dollar or even less."

The present participles have now been cut out altogether. Incidentally, I have changed the *z* of "nationalisation" to *s* simply because I prefer it that way. Some publishing houses favour *z* in such words.

For the following sentence some slight excuse may be found:

"Berlin, taking East and West together, is today the undoubted theatrical capital of Germany again, and one of the leading theatre cities of the world."

It may be argued by the writer that he meant the *taking* to be interpreted as done by Berlin. It is doubtful, however, and I should prefer this:

"East and West taken together, Berlin is today the undoubted theatrical capital of Germany . . . ."

The following is an extract from a eulogy of a leader of a nationalised industry:

"When talking to X., the future of nationalisation seems a lot more important than the past."

Surely the future of nationalisation has not been talking to X.! Yet that is just what it means. What the writer intended, of course, was this:

"When one talks to X., the future of nationalisation . . . ."

A university professor might be expected to be aware of the pitfalls in the use of participles, but here is an extract from a professor's foreword to a text-book on mining engineering:

"Having practised mining engineering for over thirty years and taught it for five, existing text-books had long seemed unsatisfactory."

If the professor wanted to use the participle he should have used it like this:

"Having practised mining engineering for over thirty years and taught it for five, I have long found existing text-books apparently unsatisfactory."

An excellent article in a scientific journal bore this title: "Exploration of the Earth's Upper Atmosphere Using High-Altitude Rockets."

Now, it was not the exploration which was using the rockets, but the experimenters. The title should have been: "Exploration of the Earth's Upper Atmosphere by the Use of High-Altitude Rockets."

UNINTENTIONAL HUMOUR

Some examples of unattached participles are unintentionally funny. Some are tragically funny, as in this extract from the transactions of a historical society:

"In carrying out this dreadful punishment, the victim was fastened into a stool or chair at the end of a sort of see-saw, and was raised and lowered into a pool of water, in which she was completely submerged . . . ."

The poor victim was not carrying out this dreadful punishment, but that is the meaning of the sentence. One way of correcting the construction would be thus:

"In the carrying-out of this dreadful punishment, the victim was fastened into a stool or chair . . . ."

This is from a reader's letter to an editor, many years ago:

"Arising out of the Suez crisis, we are about to be made to realise what it means to be short of oil and petrol, the two fuels to which some of our brilliant politicians have confined road transport."

The letter means that *we* are arising out of the Suez crisis, like Venus arising out of the foam, and it is surprising that it was published as written. The sub-editor who passed it to the compositor should have corrected it, perhaps in this fashion: "As a result of the Suez crisis, we are about to be made to realise . . . ."

A high-ranking officer in the police force wrote this in a communiqué:

"Failing to find the keys, forcible entry was effected." Did forcible entry fail to find the keys? Of course not. What the officer meant to say could have been written like this:

"Failing to find the keys, the intruders made a forcible entry," or like this clumsy alternative,

"Failure to find the keys resulted in the effecting of a forcible entry."

The following unfortunate example is from a book:

"Having eaten our dinner . . . and drunk our wines, the ladies have withdrawn and we have been left alone in the dining room."

Lest the reader may gather that the ladies were greedy, I now give the writer's intention:

"We have eaten our dinner and drunk our wines. The ladies have withdrawn and we have been left alone in the dining-room." (Notice the hyphen.)

In some chatty notes for women on Continental travel I found this gem:

"Perfume remains one of the most popular presents brought from the Continent by the returning holidaymaker. It is so popular that even after firmly declaring 'Nothing' at the Customs counter the officer is apt to fix one with a disbelieving eye and ask, 'No perfume or alcohol?'"

It is not the Customs officer who makes the declaration, however, but the traveller. The second sentence should start like this to make sense:

"It is so popular that even after one has declared 'Nothing' at the Customs counter . . . ."

UNATTACHED PAST PARTICIPLES

Most examples of the misuse of participles are concerned with present participles, which usually end in *-ing*. But even past participles, often ending in *-ed*, can lead people astray, and I shall give two examples.

The first is from a magazine concerned with motoring:

"The picnic table is within easy reach when seated on camp stools."

Logically, this means that when the picnic-table is seated on camp-stools it is within easy reach. This kind of thing takes us into a world of tiresome nonsense, for the writer does not even say that he is referring to the picnickers. No doubt what he means is this:

"The picnic-table is within easy reach when the picnickers are seated on camp-stools."

But there is no need to go to this length, and the following would be quite adequate: "The picnic-table is within easy reach of the camp-stools."

My second example is from the catalogue of a building exhibition:

"Strong, clean and economically priced, we have strong conviction in recommending this product."

Let this be the last. We have gone beyond amusement. A suitable reconstruction of this horrible example would be:

"We have strong conviction in recommending this product, which is strong, clean and cheap."

OTHER MISUSES OF THE PRESENT PARTICIPLE

There is one form of construction with the present participle which, frankly, presents a problem. I refer to the instructional or informative type of sentence which reads something like this:

"The machine is started by switching on the current and moving the control arm over to the extreme left."

This is not right as it stands, as the participles *switching* and *moving* are not disciplined by anything. The sentence would be quite correct, however, in this form:

"The operator starts the machine by switching on the current and moving the control arm over to the extreme left." Here, the participles are disciplined by the words *the operator*, which are, in fact, the subject of the sentence. In the example as given, it is difficult to analyse the sentence into subject, verb and object, and, in fact, if a sentence cannot be so analysed it is suspect.

If the example is an instruction to operators, it could just as well have been written, quite correctly, in the imperative mood:

"Start the machine by switching on the current and moving the control arm over to the extreme left."

Such sentences are not always instructions to operators, and the imperative mood cannot always be used. One solution is to treat such awkward participles as nouns, like this:

"The machine is started by the switching-on of the current and the moving of the control arm over to the extreme left."

This sentence, though correct, is clumsy. Some sentences, if treated in this way with present participles as nouns, are even worse. How, for instance, could the following be corrected?

1. "A new lawn may be made either by laying turves or by sowing seed."

2. "Cut as shown in the illustration, the centre cut being made by pressing the knife-blade down and pulling it out."

3. "There is an electronic wheel-balancing machine that enables the wheels to be balanced without removing them from the car."

4. "Any misadjustment may be gauged by grasping the centre ring firmly with both hands and pushing it down and pulling it up along the length of the shaft."

First, let us see the effect of treating the present participles as nouns.

1. "A new lawn may be made either by the laying of turves or by the sowing of seed."

2. "Cut as shown in the illustration, the centre cut being made by a pressing of the knife-blade down and a pulling of it out."

3. "There is an electronic wheel-balancing machine that enables the wheels to be balanced without the removing of them from the car."

4. "Any misadjustment may be gauged by a grasping of the centre ring firmly with both hands and a pushing of it down and a pulling of it up along the length of the shaft."

No. 1 now sounds satisfactory. Nos. 2, 3 and 4, however, are too cumbersome, and it would be better to rewrite the sentences. As No. 2 starts in the imperative mood ("Cut as shown") it might as well continue in this mood. Here are my suggestions:

2. "Cut as shown in the illustration, making the centre cut by pressing the knife-blade down and pulling it out."

3. "There is an electronic wheel-balancing machine that enables the wheels to be balanced without their removal from the car."

4. "Any misadjustment may be gauged if the centre ring is grasped firmly with both hands and pushed down and pulled up along the length of the shaft."

The present participle *being* is often maltreated, as in the following examples:

1. "The possibility of strong head winds being encountered is not precluded."

2. "The skid appears to have been precipitated by oil being sprayed on to a rear wheel by a defective oil breather pipe."

3. "Upon it being explained to him, he agreed with the proposal."

All these examples can be easily corrected by the treatment of present participles as nouns, in this way:

1. "The possibility of the encountering of strong head winds is not precluded."

2. "The skid appears to have been precipitated by the spraying of oil on to a rear wheel by a defective oil breather pipe."

4. "Upon its being explained to him, he agreed with the proposal."

Sometimes the correct manipulation of a present participle makes the sentence sound clumsy, as we have seen. But if you argue that ungrammatical sentences like those I have quoted are justified by common usage, I cannot agree. Common usage can occasionally be a good servant but is never a master. If common usage is to be our only guide in grammar we leave the way open to all kinds of slipshod writing and speech and even to illiteracy.

UNRELATED WORDS

Lastly, I come to misconstructions of sentences by the use of unrelated words other than participles.

This is from an article on a celebrated man:

"Though shy of personal publicity, most people find him friendly and easy to get on with."

This means that most people are shy of personal publicity. The writer, on the other hand, really means that the celebrated man is shy. If the writer had read the passage carefully before sending it for publication he should have realised that readers would be hoodwinked by the false relation of "Though shy" with "most people." The editorial staff were dull in not noticing the mistake, and the sentence could have been corrected simply by the insertion of "he is" after "Though."

CHAPTER XI

Oddities of the Language

‡••••••••••••••••••••••••••••••••••••••‡

In English there are numerous peculiar constructions and uses of words which cannot be classed as mistakes but which are interesting enough to deserve discussion. While many of these are acceptable in literate society, some are not recommended for regular use and may, in fact, be frowned upon.

I shall deal with some of these language oddities—as I have called them for the purpose of this chapter—and shall start with the subject of clichés.

CLICHÉS

Cliché is the past participle of the French verb *clicher*, "to stereotype." Thus, in English, a cliché is a word, phrase, clause or sentence that has become figuratively stereotyped, or so overworked that it has ceased to be effective. Clichés are often used innocently by ingenuous people and are apt to provoke tolerant smiles or, at the worst, impolite sniggers.

The thing to remember about any cliché is that originally it was a clever, pungent, economical, euphonious or even witty expression. Whoever started it, other people copied it because they liked the sound of it or because of its handiness in saving thought and in expressing much in little.

Through constant use, however, clichés lose their originality and can even become evidence of mental poverty in their users. They are to be avoided as far as possible. I say "as far as possible" because certain useful words like "incidentally" and phrases like "as a matter of fact," which are undeniable clichés, are so truly useful that they do not bring "the ghost of a smile" (this is a cliché) to the face of a listener or reader. I say "as far as possible" for a second reason—that nobody, try as he may, can avoid clichés altogether.

"Commercial English" bristles with clichés, and I appreciate a business letter written in straightforward language.

I give below a list of clichés, some of them old, some not so old. If any of these expressions, or others like them, come into your mind while you are writing or speaking, you must be cautious. In writing you have time to hunt for ways of escape, but in speech you are liable to say the first thing you think of.

"I couldn't care less."

"Prior to" (before)

"Raining cats and dogs"

"A step in the right direction"

"The arm of the law"

"Common or garden"

"Wearing-apparel"

"The order of the day"

"Leaving no stone unturned"

"Making the supreme sacrifice"

"The long arm of coincidence."

"In his heart of hearts"

"Conspicuous by his absence"

"The irony of fate"

"Not wisely but too well"

"This hurts me more than it hurts you."

"The major part of" (most of)

"I read him like a book."

"Smoking like a house on fire"

"The letter of the law"

"With monotonous regularity"

"By and large"

"Reading-matter"

"Exploring every avenue"

"Be made the recipient of" (be given).

"It stands to reason."

"Sleeping the sleep of the just"

"The cup that cheers but not inebriates"

"Leave well alone"

"The psychological moment"

"More in sorrow than anger"

"Nemesis overtook him."

You will be able to add many clichés to this list.

COMMERCIAL ENGLISH

"Commercial English," as I have said, bristles with clichés, but these clichés are of a particular and strange kind. A business letter in simple English shows that the writer has cleared his mind of, or has never acquired, those lifeless collections of words which may even, for all I know, be taught in commercial schools.

"Yours to hand," for instance—this is dreadful. "The work is in hand" is only slightly better. Then there are our old friends *inst.*, *ult.* and *prox.*, which are indefensible. There is no reason at all why dates should not be given as the 15th June or the 20th December. The horrible expression "even date," for "today," is inexplicable, for it does not even have the virtue of saving space.

"I acknowledge receipt of your letter" is ungrammatical. You receive a letter, or you acknowledge a letter, but you cannot acknowledge receipt.

So many writers of business letters think it a sin to repeat anything that they are prone to writing about "the same," or even "same." This quaint practice is so unnecessary as to be comical.

"We regret" is often used where it would be more polite or more feeling to say "We are sorry." There may be a difference between "tell" and "inform," but in cases where there is no difference "tell" is preferable.

"I would" or "we would" is often used instead of "I should" or "we should." "Forward" and "despatch" are used where "send" would be better. "Begin" or "start" is usually better than "commence." Personally, I only use the longer or the less simple word if the rhythm of the letter is improved by it.

Rock-bottom is touched by *re* and *in re*. These are especially favoured by solicitors, who should know better.

"AS TO," "AS REGARDS," "WITH REGARD TO"

"As to the children," we might read, "they are enjoying their holiday immensely."

I do not know why the writer could not have written simply: "The children are enjoying their holiday immensely." Let us suppose, however, that he had a genuine reason; for example, he might have begun writing about the other members of the family and wanted to make a special point of adding something about the children."

Instead of "As to," then, he might have used "As for," "As regards," "With regard to," or, ungrammatically, "Regarding." "Regarding" is wrong because it is an unattached present participle; the children are not regarding themselves.

Anyway, the five expressions, similar in meaning, are clumsy.

They are, however, shorter than the full and more explanatory construction:

"On the subject of the children, I can report that they are enjoying their holiday immensely."

Are the expressions acceptable? "Regarding" is not acceptable, as we have seen. "As regards" is the most awkward, for it is difficult to find any logical basis for it. "As to" and "As for" are better. "With regard to," in my opinion, is the most acceptable of all.

"THE FORMER" AND "THE LATTER"

Too much use is made of "the former" and "the latter," in the mistaken belief that it is bad English to repeat a word. It *may* be bad English if the repetition can be avoided, but the use of "the former" and "the latter" is a poor way of avoiding it.

"The two greatest men in the history of Stonechester were Emmanuel Scamper and Benjamin Thwaites. Both were staunch councillors and noted philanthropists, but while the former was noted also for his horse-racing interests the latter's aversion from all kinds of gambling was particularly well known."

When the reader comes across "the former" and "the latter" he has to look back to see what is meant, and this is one factor against their use. In the above passage, for instance, the reader cannot be expected to grasp immediately that "the former" is Scamper and "the latter" Thwaites.

"The former" and "the latter" also tend to make a passage sound stilted. I should prefer it written in this way:

"The two greatest men in the history of Stonechester were Emmanuel Scamper and Benjamin Thwaites. Both were staunch councillors and noted philanthropists, but while Scamper was noted also for his horse-racing interests Thwaites's aversion from all kinds of gambling was particularly well known."

"Aversion from," incidentally, is right. The common "aversion to" is wrong, "to" (as I have explained elsewhere) signifying approach.

I know that everybody uses "the former" and "the latter" sometimes, but their use should be minimised and confined as far as possible to complicated items consisting of groups of words. One important thing to remember is that "the former" and "the latter" can be used only for a *pair* of items, and the following examples are wrong:

"Problems of the future which will have to be faced by our big cities include housing of increasing populations, provision of more schools, smooth and balanced organisation of public transport, and long-overdue elimination of traffic congestion. Of these problems, the former is perhaps the most urgent."

"Speaking of Marlowe, Bacon and Shakespeare himself, I think there is no doubt that the latter was responsible for all the plays."

In the first example, the use of "the former" would be quite justified if there had been only two items, as each item consists of a group of words which could not be conveniently repeated. As there are more than two items, however, it is wrong to use "the former," and in such cases we should say "the first" and "the last" or "the first-named" and "the last-named."

In the second example "the last" or "the last-named" should have been used if this kind of construction had been wanted, but the sentence would be better in this form:

"Speaking of Marlowe, Bacon and Shakespeare, I think there is no doubt that Shakespeare himself was responsible for all the plays."

ELLIPSIS IN COMPARISONS

Ellipsis (page 53) is simply a shortening by the omission of certain words which are understood, and by "ellipsis in comparisons" I mean sentences like this:

"Temperatures today will be lower than yesterday." This is a shortened form of each of the following:

"Temperatures today will be lower than yesterday's."

"Temperatures today will be lower than they were yesterday."

"Temperatures today will be lower than those of yesterday."

The ellipsis is generally acceptable, but I think it preferable to use the full form if it is not too unwieldy.

SWITCHED ADJECTIVES

When we speak of a "generous gift" we do not mean that the gift is generous but that the giver is generous. The adjective *generous* has been switched from one thing to another and becomes a "switched adjective."

There is no harm in this practice as long as the reader or listener understands the intention of the writer or speaker. Other examples of switched adjectives are "glad tidings," "sad news" and even "happy Christmas."

"LOST TO"

The phrase *lost to* is strangely used in two ways, as the following sentences show:

"When Mr. X. retired from business after fifty years of hard work he felt that the commercial world was lost to him for ever."

"When Mr. X. played in the bowls match this year he lost the championship to Mr. Y."

In each case it is Mr. X. who is the loser, but while in the first instance the thing lost (the commercial world) is lost to himself, in the second instance the thing lost (the championship) is lost to somebody else.

The general conclusion seems to be that if the thing lost is not gained by anyone else in particular it is *lost to* the loser. If the thing lost is gained by somebody it is *lost to* the gainer.

Here are some more examples:

"All that she had cherished was lost to her."

"Ruritania's once-prosperous trade in string bags has been lost to her go-ahead neighbour, Petularia."

"As he wandered through the streets of London, destitute, he bitterly resented the way his fortune had dwindled away and was now completely lost to him."

"As he wandered through the streets of London, destitute, he bitterly resented the way his legitimate fortune had been lost to his cunning and malevolent kinsman."

When the phrase *lose to* is used (instead of *lost to*) the thing lost can *only* be lost to the gainer:

"You must not lose your business to that terrible shop across the road."

"SPOLIATION"

Spoliation (wartime plundering, robbery or destruction) is the noun of the verb "to spoil" or "to despoil." Some people imagine that it is a corrupt form of "spoilation," but this is not so. Actually, *spoil* is the word at fault, as the Latin verb is *spoliare.*

Even if "spoilation" had been correct popular speech would probably have corrupted it to "spoliation," which is easier to say, just as popular speech has corrupted the pronunciation of *aeration* to "areation."

"AS FROM"

Two prepositions side by side are often frowned upon, but "as from" can be a useful and legitimate phrase.

"Order of 25th January, 19—. As from 1st January, wages and salaries will be increased by 5 per cent."

"As from" here indicates precisely that the order takes effect from a date earlier than the date on which it is written, and I have no quarrel with anyone who uses it in this sense. But I see no point in its use if, for example, the effective date is *after* the date of the order, in which case "as" should be omitted:

"Order of 25th January, 19—. From 1st February, wages and salaries will be increased by 5 per cent."

If we come to another kind of writing, there is this:

"He heard a voice as from a great distance, and, waking from his dream, saw his father beside him."

There is nothing wrong with "as from" if it is regarded as an ellipsis. Thus in the first example it could be "as [if it is] from," and in the last example "as [if it came] from."

LATIN ABBREVIATIONS

Etc. or *&c.* is an abbreviation of "etcetera," which is Latin for "and the rest." It should have no place in ordinary prose and its use should be confined to notes and jottings. If, after giving a list of items, a writer wants to imply the existence of more, he should use some such expression as "and so forth," "and so on," or "and others."

Other Latin abbreviations include *et al.* (*et alibi*, "and elsewhere," or *et alii*, "and others") and *et seq.* (*et sequens*, "and the following"). Note the original meaning of *alibi.*

"AND/OR"

The term "and/or" has appeared for many years not only in official publications but also in more general writing. It may be convenient in certain limited circumstances, but it is not good English.

"*Instructions to Council.* The presentation of the Aldermen to His Grace will be made by the Lord Mayor and/or the Sheriff."

Now, in that official instruction, where brevity and clarity are both desirable, I think that "and/or" is justified. There is no justification, however, for "and/or" in the following:

"The features we look for in the ideal novel include accurate characterisation, an attractive literary style, the power of holding the reader's attention, a reasonable degree of probability and/or a good plot skilfully woven."

The writer means that if we cannot have a reasonable degree of probability we want a good plot skilfully woven, but preferably we should have both. He should say so, then. It will take longer, but the reader does not expect to find telegram economy in his prose. One way of expressing the writer's intentions would be like this:

"The features we look for in the ideal novel include accurate characterisation, an attractive literary style and the power of holding the reader's attention. We also look for a reasonable degree of probability, with the addition or alternative of a good plot skilfully woven."

Here is another example:

"I should be obliged if you would kindly send me all your books, manuscripts and/or typescripts for examination."

This would be more pleasing thus:

"I should be obliged if you would kindly send me, for examination, all your books and scripts (whether manuscript or typescript)."

"LITTLE" AND "A LITTLE"

There is a distinct difference between the following two sentences:

"He had little difficulty in finding the address."

"He had a little difficulty in finding the address."

The first means that he found the address easily. The second means that he did not find it easily. The little word *a* makes all the difference, but this is just one of the funny things about English.

"TO BUILD"

The verb "to build" means "to erect." And yet we read about various things being built which are not built at all—things like tunnels, canals, and underground shelters, which are dug or (if we want a longer word) excavated.

If you are tempted to use the word *build*, therefore, stop to ask yourself if you are doing right or wrong.

POSSESSIVE PROBLEMS

Several place-names are prefixed by "Saint" or "St." Strictly, the name of the saint in each case where possession is implied should be given an apostrophe-*s*, as the place is supposed to be *his* place. There are other places, of course, where no possession is implied—St. Asaph in Wales, for example—but these present no problem of apostrophe.

Unfortunately, the official names, no doubt as adopted by the town councils, do not always follow the rules of grammar, and the resulting inconsistency must be confusing to foreigners. It is especially distressing that St. Andrew's, one of our oldest university towns, is officially St. Andrews.

The following are the *official* names of some of the "St." places in English-speaking countries: St. Abb's Head, St. Albans, St. Andrews, St. Anne's, St. Bees, St. Bride's Bay, St. Catherines (Ontario), St. Catherine's Point, St. Davids, St. Fillans, St. George's Channel, St. Helens, St. Ives, St. John's (Newfoundland), St. Leonards, St. Mary's (Scilly Isles), St. Neots.

PROBLEMS OF PLURALS

We may be confronted with alternatives of the following kinds:

"The United States are important allies."

"The United States is an important ally."

"The Straits of Gibraltar were crowded with vessels."

"The Straits of Gibraltar was crowded with vessels."

"Ten thousand tons of ore were produced in the month."

"Ten thousand tons of ore was produced in the month."

It is commonly accepted practice to treat the United States as singular, so that the first example should be:

"The United States is an important ally."

The Straits of Gibraltar, on the other hand, are treated as plural, so that here we should say:

"The Straits of Gibraltar were crowded with vessels."

Quantities expressed in tons, and in all other units, are treated as singular, the point being that it is the substance which is grammatically significant, not the number of units. Thus, in "tons of ore," the governing word is "ore," not "tons," so that the sentence should be:

"Ten thousand tons of ore was produced in the month." If, however, both the units and the substance are plural, it is natural to say (for example), "Six pounds of peas are wanted," or "Twelve acres of daffodils were destroyed by frost."

Plural problems of a different kind arise with collective nouns like *company, committee, board, society* and so forth. Do we say "The committee is agreed" or "The committee are agreed"?

There is no rule about this, and procedure largely depends on the sense. If the sense implies—as it usually does—that the company, committee, board or society *as a whole* is involved, the singular form of the verb should be used, as in the following two examples:

"The Board in its annual report has shown a profit for the year, in spite of serious strikes and increased costs."

"The Company has decided in the interests of safety to install special protective devices in the factory."

But if the sense implies that the *individual members* of the organisation are involved, the plural of the verb should be used, as in the following two examples:

"After prolonged deliberations the Committee were unanimously agreed that the scheme should be adopted."

"Following recent criticism an extraordinary meeting of the Society was held on the 31st August. At first there was considerable evidence that the Society were divided among themselves. After some discussion, however, and the reading of supporting letters from representative bodies of kindred societies, it was decided that there was no substance in the unfavourable allegations. The meeting closed with the Society convinced of their unity."

"MESSRS."

"Messrs." is the abbreviation of the French "Messieurs," or "Gentlemen." As such, it is a plural, so that Messrs. J. & A. Smith means the combination of Mr. J. Smith and Mr. A. Smith.

But once Messrs. J. & A. Smith form themselves into a limited company, perhaps under the name of J. & A. Smith Ltd., they become a *single legal person*. It is therefore incorrect to address the firm as Messrs. J. & A. Smith Ltd.

The rule is simple. "Messrs." should not be used in addressing a limited company. For a company which is not limited it should only be used if the title of the company includes a surname or surnames. Thus, you would be correct in writing "Messrs. J. & A. Smith" or "Messrs. Robinson & Co.," but you would be wrong in writing "Messrs. The Apex Jamjar Co." or "Messrs. Happifoot Shoes." Letters addressed to the last two firms would be inscribed "The Apex Jamjar Co." and "Happifoot Shoes."

"SCOTCH," "SCOTTISH," "SCOTS"

Do not imagine that "Scotch" is a vulgarism, or, in the facetious words of some Englishmen, "only the name of a drink." Reputable Scotch writers up to the nineteenth century, notably Burns and Scott, were not afraid of the adjective "Scotch," although natives of Scotland could be called Scotsmen.

"Scottish" may be the older form and seems to be generally favoured by many English people, perhaps to distinguish it from the verb "to scotch" and perhaps from a mistaken fancy that "Scotch" sounds inelegant.

Attempts have been made to effect a compromise by the use of "Scots" as an adjective. These attempts certainly have historical and literary validity, but one objection to "Scots" is the possibility of awkwardness if, for instance, it should be mistaken for the possessive "Scot's" (singular) or the possessive "Scots'" (plural). Thus, the title of the excellent *Scots Magazine* never was meant to imply that the magazine belonged to or was published for Scots (Scotsmen and Scotswomen) but that it was the Scottish or Scotch magazine.

SCOTTISH USAGE

Some Scots use certain words and phrases in ways which sound peculiar to many English people unfamiliar with Scotch usage. On page 53, for example, I referred to the commendable adoption of "amn't I?" for "am I not?" (instead of the horrible English "aren't I?"). On the whole, the Scots are better grammarians than the English, and most of their linguistic curiosities, when examined, are found to be technically sound.

Notes on a few examples of Scotch usage will now follow.

"Presently"

There is a distinct difference in meaning between the Englishman's *presently* and the Scotsman's. In England it means "soon, in a little while." In Scotland it means "at present, now, at this very moment." Thus to people of either nation, unused to their neighbours' habits, it can lead to misunderstanding.

When a Scotsman, in a business letter, writes, "We are dealing with the matter presently," he means that his firm are dealing with the matter at the moment, but the English recipients of the letter would conclude that the matter was to be dealt with in a short while.

Yet, strangely, the legal language of both countries still gives *presently* its Scottish meaning, and you can find it used in this way in numerous legal documents.

"Mistress"

The title "Mrs." is an abbreviation of "Mistress," but only among some old-fashioned Scots will you hear the abbreviation pronounced as "Mistress." The usual pronunciation of "Mrs." is the only way of distinguishing the meaning of the word as a title from its other meanings.

"What like"

Englishmen will say "What is the park like?" Some Scotsmen will say "What like is the park?"

There is nothing wrong with this syntax. Indeed, where there is some distance between the Englishman's "What is" and "like" the Scottish practice has much to commend it. Thus, "What like are the gardens at the other end of the park?" is much neater than "What are the gardens at the other end of the park like?"

"Purpose"

"I purpose to apply for permission next week" used to be both English and Scotch usage, but now the use of *purpose* for *propose* is found mainly in Scotland.

"Retiral"

In England a man speaks of his "retirement," but in Scotland he speaks of his "retiral."

"Shock"

While, medically, *shock* in England means something definite, in Scotland it has an additional meaning, the meaning of *stroke*. Thus, "He died of a stroke" in England would be "He died of a shock" among some Scots.

"Outwith"

Outwith is sometimes used by Scotsmen for *outside*, as in the sentence, "The subject is outwith the committee's terms of reference."

Ellipsis

I said that most Scottish linguistic curiosities were technically sound, but this remark does not apply to the habit of unjustified ellipsis (omission of certain words). Some Scots may say "Have you plenty money?" when they mean "Have you plenty of money?" They may say "He wants in" instead of "He wants to come in," or "He wants out" instead of "He wants to go out."

A fairly common example of such ellipsis is, "She said to tell you to come home," instead of "She said I was to tell you to come home."

SCOTLAND

Having dealt with the adjectives "Scotch," "Scottish" and "Scots," and with Scottish usage, I feel I should conclude by dealing with Scotland itself. Though not a Scot I have Scotch sympathies; I appreciate accuracy, and it annoys me to hear English people refer to "England" when they mean Great Britain or the United Kingdom. The Press is not immune from the vice, and I have even read of "the island of England."

Use "England" and "English" when you mean "England" and "English." Use "Wales" and "Welsh" when you mean precisely these things. Use "Scotland" and "Scotch" (or "Scottish" or "Scots") when these are the words you really mean.

But when you mean "Britain"and "British" you must use "Britain" and "British." Just as my own county of Yorkshire is only part of England, England is only part of Britain, and failure to recognise the existence of the smaller British countries is a sign of ignorance, thoughtlessness, "little-Englishness," parochialism or bad manners.

INTRUDERS

Since this book first appeared—in 1958—English has been invaded by many unwelcome intruders in the form of debased usages. Additions to or modifications of a language can be necessary, logical, mellifluous or all three. Such innovations are healthy and welcome, but there are others which, being unnecessary, illogical or discordant, are certainly unwelcome. Examples spring to the mind.

The word *like*, which has several legitimate uses, is now often misused in ways that offend the ear. It is commonly substituted for *as*, as in "Like I said," "It should offend him like it offends me." Some misusages are so grotesque that only complete reconstruction would rectify the offending passages. Thus, a woman publisher (of all people!), interviewed about her interests, is reported to have said: "I've several, like I go to the theatre a lot."

Here are other examples of strange construction which, if you are sensitive about English, will make you wince:

"At this point in time" for "now" or "at present."

"Overly" instead of a simple "over," as in "over-anxious."

"For real" and "for free" instead of "real" and "free."

"From whence" instead of "whence" (literally "where from?").

"But" for emphasis, as in: "It was disastrous, *but* disastrous."

If you are interested enough to read this book you must care about your language, but there are not enough people like you. You should avoid pedantry and primness but maintain constant vigilance.

Epilogue

THOUGH we have come to the end of our book we have certainly not exhausted the study of English. The grammar of a language is not very flexible, and differs little from one generation to another. Idioms and usage are more flexible, changing not only from age to age but also from county to county. The vocabulary of a language, however, is undergoing constant change. Words change in meaning, words in different parts of a country acquire different meanings, and new words are introduced from year to year. Ralph Waldo Emerson, in *Letters and Social Aims*, truly said: "Language is a city, to the building of which every human being brought a stone." Words can form a most engrossing study, and I hope that I have been able to stimulate your interest in them.

Before I close I want to give you some advice on three matters.

First, I advise you to write simply, avoiding clichés (about which I wrote in the last chapter) and circumlocutions. (A circumlocution is something said a long way round.) I advise you to avoid "commercial English," all forms of padding, and the strange obscurity which turns a rat-catcher into a rodent operative.

Second, you should be sparing in the use of foreign words and phrases. A foreign word or phrase may be used if there is no exactly suitable word or phrase in English, or, occasionally, if it effects an economy in writing. If you use too many alien expressions you may offend the reader who does not know what they mean.

Lastly, you should be careful with quotations. If you are not sure of the exact words of a quoted author you should not grudge the time spent in checking. Shakespeare's line from *The Merchant of Venice*, "All that glisters is not gold," is often misquoted as "All is not gold that glitters," and one year the misquotation even appeared in a literary year book.

I have enjoyed writing these collections of notes and hope that you will enjoy reading them. I dare to hope, moreover, that you will read them with profit and develop a new consciousness of the language.

INDEX

185

SAMPLE SOCIAL SPEECHES

WIT, STORIES, JOKES, ANECDOTES, EPIGRAMS, Etc.

Gordon Williams

At last!

The book the world has waited for.

Gordon Williams, brilliant British speaker, has worked out a technique based on numerous specimen speeches, to enable *you* to use them to build up your social speech.

He has given you many samples on which you can base a fresh new talk or speech of your own. You can add to it with gay or serious stories from his unique selection, or "salt" it with one or more of his jokes, epigrams and witticisms.

Britain is the home of Public Speakers: F. E. Smith, Aneurin Bevan and Winston Churchill are now part of our history, but in every sphere of life where speaking counts, Britain, or, more accurately, England, leads.

Uniform with this volume

Elliot Right Way Books

Kingswood, Surrey, U.K.

HOW GOOD IS YOUR ENGLISH?

TEST YOURSELF AND SEE

By Cedric Astle, B.A. (Hons.)

No matter how good you *think* your English is, there are bound to be things you do not know.

With this book you can test your knowledge of every aspect of the English language. Vocabulary, meanings, spellings, pronunciations, derivations, grammar, punctuation, literature and others.

If you can answer every question correctly, then your English is superb. Even if you can only answer a small proportion correctly first time, your English may still be very good and with this book you will have a lot of fun improving it in the process.

Uniform with this book

ELLIOT RIGHT WAY BOOKS
KINGSWOOD, SURREY, U.K.

OUR PUBLISHING POLICY

HOW WE CHOOSE

Our policy is to consider every deserving manuscript and we can give special editorial help where an author is an authority on his subject but an inexperienced writer. We are rigorously selective in the choice of books we publish. We set the highest standards of editorial quality and accuracy. This means that a *Paperfront* is easy to understand and delightful to read. Where illustrations are necessary to convey points of detail, these are drawn up by a subject specialist artist from our panel.

HOW WE KEEP PRICES LOW

We aim for the big seller. This enables us to order enormous print runs and achieve the lowest price for you. Unfortunately, this means that you will not find in the *Paperfront* list any titles on obscure subjects of minority interest only. These could not be printed in large enough quantities to be sold for the low price at which we offer this series.

We sell almost all our *Paperfronts* at the same unit price. This saves a lot of fiddling about in our clerical departments and helps us to give you world-beating value. Under this system, the longer titles are offered at a price which we believe to be unmatched by any publisher in the world.

OUR DISTRIBUTION SYSTEM

Because of the competitive price, and the rapid turnover, *Paperfronts* are possibly the most profitable line a bookseller can handle. They are stocked by the best bookshops all over the world. It may be that your bookseller has run out of stock of a particular title. If so, he can order more from us at any time—we have a fine reputation for "same day" despatch, and we supply any order, however small (even a single copy), to any bookseller who has an account with us. We prefer you to buy from your bookseller, as this reminds him of the strong underlying public demand for *Paperfronts*. Members of the public who live in remote places, or who are housebound, or whose local bookseller is unco-operative, can order direct from us by post.

FREE

If you would like an up-to-date list of all paperfront titles currently available, send a stamped self-addressed envelope to
ELLIOT RIGHT WAY BOOKS, BRIGHTON RD.,
LOWER KINGSWOOD, SURREY, U.K.